BRIGHT STAR

BY CONSTANCE FECHER

VENTURE FOR A CROWN

HEIR TO PENDARROW

BRIGHT STAR: A PORTRAIT OF ELLEN TERRY

Constance Fecher

BRIGHT STAR

A PORTRAIT OF ELLEN TERRY

Farrar, Straus & Giroux · New York

AN ARIEL BOOK

First printing, 1970

Library of Congress catalog card number: 70–125151
SBN 374.3.0965.5
Printed in the United States of America
Designed by Judith Lerner
Published simultaneously in Canada
by Doubleday Canada Ltd., Toronto

GRATEFUL ACKNOWLEDGMENTS are due to the following for permission to quote: to Gilbert Samuel & Company, literary executors for Ellen Terry, for quotations from *Memoirs,* edited by Edith Craig and Christopher St. John; to the Society of Authors for the quotation from *Dramatic Opinions and Essays* by George Bernard Shaw; to Hamish Hamilton Limited, for quotations from *Time Was* by W. Graham Robertson; to London Management and Victor Gollancz Limited, for quotations from *Gordon Craig* by Edward Craig; to Studio Vista Limited, for the quotation from *Index to the Story of My Days* by Gordon Craig.

for my sister
WINIFRED

Contents

Preface

"HOW IS IT POSSIBLE to describe to a generation who knows her not the beauty of Ellen Terry?" wrote the artist W. Graham Robertson, and he was right. To conjure an actress out of the darkness of the past is a difficult task. Acting is such a transient art. It is not like a book or a picture or a poem. There is nothing tangible. In the theatre, with an audience on which she can play as a musician plays on his instrument, an actress is supreme, all-powerful. The play is the thing and the spoken words spring to magical life. But when the curtain comes down, there is nothing left, only a name on a program, faded flowers, a dusty costume hanging forlornly on a peg in an empty dressing room. She lives for us only in the memories of those who saw her in her moments of glory, and yet how fragrant some of those memories can be.

There are some among the great players of the past whose story lingers on, not merely because of their ability to create the characters they played but because they themselves in their own persons possessed some imperishable quality. Such a one was Ellen Terry.

She charmed audiences for more than fifty years in England, America, and Australia. She wrote her own story, vividly, unforgettably, recording her thoughts, her feelings, her experiences in the theatre, her generous judgments of her fellow players. She could laugh at herself as well as cry. She was without vanity or conceit. "To be useful in the theatre—is ever the height of my ambition," she wrote once. Yet, during the twenty-five years she reigned with Henry Irving at the Lyceum, she became the darling, the idol of the English audiences, a legend in her own lifetime.

Though I have told her story in dramatic form, every event related actually took place, the thoughts and opinions of the characters are their own, the conversations except for an occasional linking phrase are all drawn from her own memoirs and from the letters and reminiscences of friends and acquaintances. In this way I have endeavored to bring her to life, warm and vital as she really was, with her children, her dogs, and her great friend and fellow artist, Sir Henry Irving.

BRIGHT STAR

1

Child of the Theatre

DECEMBER IS A BLEAK cold month in Scotland. Bitter winds come raging up the river Clyde from the Irish Sea, freezing the puddles and whipping the snow in the streets of Glasgow into great drifts.

Inside the Theatre Royal, icy drafts swirled across the stage. Impatiently the actors stamped their feet, huddled into their mufflers and greatcoats. At this rate, the pantomime rehearsal was likely to go on till the evening performance, with no chance for snatching a meal or a cup of something hot. The actors glared furiously at the cause of the trouble.

The small girl stood stubbornly, sturdy legs apart, the bonnet pushed back from her shock of yellow curls, blue eyes defiant.

"Put your child into the mustard pot, Mr. Terry!" yelled the exasperated producer.

Her father looked at her appealingly, but Ellen shook her head. It would be dark in there, like being shut in a cupboard, like the narrow passage running under the stage from one side to the other with its black beetles. Even the thought of the yellow gauzy dress, the fun of popping out like a jack-in-the-box as the Spirit of the Mustard Pot to the shrieking delight of the audience, couldn't take away the terror. She screwed up her eyes, the round cheeks puckered, and she burst into loud and noisy sobs.

"Damn you and your mustard pot, sir!" exploded her father. "I'll not frighten my child for you or anyone!" He clapped his hat on his head, seized Ellen by the hand, glared at his fellow actors, and defiantly strode out of the theatre.

Stumbling after him through the slippery, slushy streets, her face still smudged and wet with tears, Ellen knew he was both angry and disappointed. He had great ambitions for his children and this was the first part she had ever been asked to play.

Glasgow houses are black and narrow and very tall. Their lodgings were far away on the top floor. The stone stairs seemed as high as a mountain and Ellen's short legs ached as she toiled after her father. She was not quite four years old.

The large attic room, when they reached it at last, glowed cheerfully in the warm light of the fire. There was a delicious smell of grilling herrings. Fish was cheap in the market down by the river. Young though she was, Ellen knew that money was always scarce and every penny had to be carefully spent.

Her mother asked a question and her father shook his head. Her brother, Benjamin, who was nearly twelve, was sprawled on the hearthrug. He gave a snort of laughter. Kate, toasting fork in hand, turned a flushed, scornful face and stuck her pert nose in the air. Kate had danced a hornpipe on the stage when she was only three and now at seven was an experienced actress whose weekly salary helped them to live.

Ellen didn't care. She was kicking off her soaked boots and thrusting out frozen toes to the warmth of the fire. She grimaced hideously at Kate and thrust out a defiant pink tongue.

"Nellie!" Her mother shook her head reprovingly at her, but then her father had swung her around to face him, wagging a stern finger in front of her nose. "You'll never make an actress, Nellie, never!" he said severely, and stood her in the corner.

She endured it for a little. Then the clatter of teacups, the appetizing smell of the herrings was too much. Big tears began to ooze out of the blue eyes and roll down her cheeks. Ben Terry was too good-natured, he loved his children too well, to be harsh with them for long. Besides, Nellie, his "Duchess" as he called her, had always been his favorite despite her willful ways.

Presently they were all crowded around the table. The fish disappeared in no time, but there was plenty of bread, with a scrape of butter or jam, and cups of hot sweet tea, and Ben had them in gales of laughter at his imitation of the producer's rage, Nellie's defiance, and the disgust of the actors.

Then it was time for them to go to the theatre. Her mother brought out the mattress from under the big bed, unfolding the blankets while Ellen pulled the brown serge frock over her head and unbuttoned the red flannelette petticoat, shivering in her long cotton knickers. Kate would share the mattress with her when they all came back after the evening performance. George, who was only a baby, was too young to be left behind. Wrapped snugly in his thick shawl, he would sleep peacefully in a corner of her mother's dressing room, as Ellen herself had done only a year or so ago.

Tucked up in blankets, reminded to be a good girl and not

to get up or touch the fire, Ellen saw them leave and heard the key turn in the lock. She was not frightened. An actor's child soon learns to sleep alone in different rooms. She lay watching the firelight quiver over the ceiling, turning the brass knobs of the big bed into balls of gold, until her eyes, following a dancing shadow on the walls, fell on the oak bureau pulled close under the high window.

She was an adventurous child. She scrambled up from the mattress, tripping over the hem of her long flannel nightgown, climbed onto a chair, then onto the bureau, and pulled aside the dusty plush curtain. She caught her breath in rapture.

It was so unexpected, so wonderful. A fiery red winter sun like a huge orange was sinking into gray mists. Gold, pink, and flame turned the clouds into fairy castles. Entranced, she watched until it changed into green and violet and primrose, and when it had all faded, out of the darkness there flared pin-points of light, like torches, like the sparks shooting upward from a forge where she had once watched the horses of the stagecoach being shod. She pressed her face against the icy glass, small chilblained fingers rubbing at the film already forming on the window. She was seeing the flaming glory of a sunset for the first time. It both terrified and fascinated her.

Ellen's fourth birthday would not be until after Christmas, on February 27. Her parents, Ben and Sarah Terry, were strolling players and she was born when they were playing at Coventry in 1847, ten years after the Princess Victoria had succeeded to the English throne at the age of eighteen.

Sometimes Ben would tell his children about the glories of the Coronation celebrations in Portsmouth, where he and Sarah had grown up. Portsmouth had been a naval base since the time of the Romans, he told them proudly. Lord Nelson had sailed from there in 1805 to win the battle of Trafalgar and save England from Napoleon. The great sailing ships still crowded the harbor when he was a boy, though now they were giving way to ironclad steamships, ugly black monsters, not to be compared in grace and lightness with the tall tea clippers racing across the Atlantic to the China seas.

But then Ben Terry was romantic, a tall, handsome, brown-haired man with Irish blood in his veins. Ellen adored her gay, charming, amusing father. He would tell her what a lively town Portsmouth was when the fleet was in. Sailors crowded the inns down by the harbor, spending lavishly the wages they had earned on their year-long voyages. The straw on the alehouse floors used to be carefully sifted through, each morning, for the pieces of gold dropped by careless fingers during the drinking of the night before.

Ben and his brother, her uncle George, would thump the drum and play the fiddle to amuse the customers at his widowed mother's tavern, the Fortune of War. The sailors would stamp their feet and shout for song after song. Brother George played the violin in the tiny barnlike theatre, and that Coronation Year when it reopened, Ben and his drum went to join the theatre orchestra. "That's the way to learn!" he would say impressively to Kate and Ellen listening wide-eyed.

Night after night across the flickering oil lamps that served as footlights, he had watched the players in everything from Shakespeare down to the crudest melodrama, till he knew everyone's part by heart. He helped to build the scenery, he painted canvas flats, he swept the stage, he ran errands, and told Sarah all about it when they went walking together on Sunday afternoons.

Here he would stop and smile at their mother across the tea table, for the course of true love had not run smooth for them. Sarah Ballard's father was a builder and also a lay preacher;

her mother came from a sound, respectable Scottish family. Both her parents disapproved of the good-looking gay young man, with his passionate desire to become an actor, with no money and no prospects, even though he dutifully attended the Wesleyan Chapel with his mother every Sunday morning.

He was not the son-in-law they wanted. They would have preferred her to marry one of the well-off young tradesmen who came courting their beautiful daughter, but Sarah had fallen deeply in love. She refused all her suitors and continued to meet Ben secretly, listening to his dreams till she believed in them herself. Then one day he confided to her that when the players left the town to go on tour he was going with them, this time as an actor. He was bursting with pride. It was a wonderful opportunity. She could not resist the pleading in the brown eyes. She could not let him leave without her.

That Coronation Year they both had reached the age of twenty-one and could defy her parents' wishes. On a golden September morning in 1838 they were secretly married and left Portsmouth in a postchaise, the last merry fling of Ben's remaining few shillings and never regretted it, never for a single moment, he would say triumphantly.

What he did not speak of, simply because it never even occurred to him to do so, was how hard those first years had been. They were young and in love and on fresh spring mornings or in cool summer dawns it could be good fun to ride on the baggage cart or tramp the country roads from one small town to the next. In those early days of mid-century the newly built railways only linked the larger towns, and in any case the fare was far too expensive for their limited means, and riding in the open wagons gritty with cinders underfoot, you ended up filthy and covered in black smuts.

When the rains came or the winter snows, it could be bitterly cold and exhausting even if enough money could be scraped together for a seat on the stagecoach. The theatres they played in were often no more than small barns. Lodging-house keepers were not anxious to provide food or fires for these hard-up travelers who could afford only the cheapest rooms.

The women in the company would gather on the stage or in tiny dressing rooms, sometimes alive with vermin, sometimes with snow or rain leaking through the roof, and always the smell of mice and drains and sickly stale perfume from dusty makeup boxes. There they would cook their food, sew and mend their costumes, learn their parts, and teach the children the alphabet while the menfolk tramped the streets advertising the show they would put on that very night.

If Sarah ever regretted her comfortable home with its fine mahogany furniture and polished floors, its fourposter bed with the lavender-scented sheets and handsome patchwork quilt, she never spoke of it. She adored her young husband, who was everyone's favorite and already winning golden praise for his acting.

She called herself Miss Yerret (Terry spelled backward) and taught herself to walk on in the plays and even to act small parts, and because she was gentle and always willing to help, she was well liked among her husband's friends. She was skillful with her needle and made her own clothes and the children's too when they came. She was a wonderful mother. She and Ben between them had the happy gift of creating a warm and loving home for Benjamin and Kate and Ellen wherever they went.

By the time Ellen was born, they had already begun to rise in their profession. Ben was being offered better parts. He was lucky enough to get several months in a good stock company, playing in *Martin Chuzzlewit*, adapted from a novel by a Mr. Charles Dickens, who was also born in Portsmouth and who was now a very successful author indeed, vastly enjoying himself in private theatricals and showing off his embroidered waistcoats and varnished boots in London.

That was where they would all be one day, Ben would declare. That was his ambition, and his determination never wavered. It was a bitter disappointment to him that Benjamin, their first-born, had no aptitude and no liking for the stage. For all his teaching, the boy could not get one line into his thick head. But there was Kate, who was so precociously clever. He pinned great hopes on her. And now there was Nellie.

Her mother sighed sometimes when she thought of Nellie. She was sweet-tempered enough, but so careless, so untidy. Even as a baby, she had tried to run before she could walk. She was always rushing into things and coming to disaster. You had to have eyes all around you to keep Nellie out of mischief. Kate was her comfort. She was so steady and serious and hard-working. Just what Sarah had been brought up to be, and the ideal she wanted for all her children.

Ellen was back in bed and fast asleep when they came home from the theatre, all of them tired and chilled to the bone. She woke up when Kate climbed into the bed and two small frozen feet landed in the small of her back, but then there was the comfort of the hot flannel-wrapped brick which had been warming in the hearth, and through sleepy, half-closed eyes, Ellen watched her mother brush the long silky light-brown hair and weave it into a loose plait.

Sarah was tall and graceful. In the candlelight in her long white petticoats, her little daughter thought she looked beautiful. Then the light was blown out, the big bed creaked, and Ellen stretched up a small hand. This was something she did every night. With her father's strong warm fingers clasped around her own, she closed her eyes and contentedly went back to sleep.

"*You spotted snakes, with double tongue,*
Thorny hedge-hogs, be not seen . . ."

"Go on, Nellie," urged Ben.

Ellen looked down at her bread and milk longingly and then at the spoon held firmly in her father's hand. It was breakfast time, but lessons had to be repeated before she would be allowed to eat. A battered copy of Shakespeare had been her first reading book. He had been teaching her the lines from *A Midsummer Night's Dream* all that week.

"Newts and blind-worms . . ." went on Ellen, and stopped. What was a blind-worm? Was it a kind of snake, and how did it see to move about and find food? And whatever was it that came next?

Her father tapped the table impatiently. Benjamin was solidly munching toast. Kate snorted scornfully into her cup of milk and water.

Her mother said gently, "Come along now, Nellie. Think, dear, think hard."

Then it all came back with a rush.

"*Newts, and blind-worms, do no wrong;*
Come not near our fairy queen.
Philomel, with melody
Sing in our sweet lullaby."

She finished it triumphantly in one breathless gabble and seized the spoon, digging it joyfully into the bread and milk.

"Consonants," reminded her father severely. "Remember your consonants. D . . . D . . . D . . . T . . . T . . . T . . . Tongue behind teeth."

"D . . . D . . . D . . . T . . . T . . . T . . ." repeated Ellen through a spray of milk. She had lost two front teeth in the last few weeks. The breakfast table went into a roar of laughter. There was always a great deal of merriment in the Terry lodgings.

Ben was determined that his children should speak beautifully. He was proud of his own fine elocution. Macready had praised it once when he had played in a stock season with him. It was the custom then for well-known actors going on tour in the provinces to play with the resident company. Macready had become Ben's idol. He spoke of him constantly as the greatest actor in all England. Sometimes Kate and Ellen grew tired of hearing about the famous William Charles Macready who last year at the age of fifty-eight had made his final bow to the public at Drury Lane.

Sarah, who on one never-to-be-forgotten day had played Gertrude to Macready's Hamlet, could have told a different story. He might be conscientious, very much in earnest, and a magnificent speaker, but he was also a snob and a great deal of a prig and he was apt to fall into violent rages and sulks. Fanny Kemble, niece to the great Mrs. Siddons, once said, "He growls and prowls and roams and foams about the stage in all directions like a tiger in his cage."

Sarah had taken his hand when he did not wish it, and he had flung her off so roughly that she was bruised from head to foot. Nevertheless, she would have agreed with Ben that there was not another tragedian at the present time to touch him.

It was a year since they had played at Glasgow. Now it was winter again and in November mists and fogs come rolling up the Mersey and blow in wisps and shreds over the Liverpool docks.

Ellen had shot up in a year. She was going to be tall like her mother and already she overtopped Kate. She had learned a great deal too. There was no schooling for actors' children moving from town to town as they did, but her father taught her to read and write and none of Sarah's children was allowed to be idle. While Kate rehearsed or learned lines, Ellen was taught to cook breakfast, to wash and scrub, and to roast a joint for dinner. She was always good with baby George. She would love to help bathe him, making him crow with laughter at her antics and inventing games while she rubbed his mop of flaxen curls dry.

What she hated more than anything was learning to sew or darn the never-ending holes in the woolen stockings. She escaped whenever she could.

Sarah still worried about her. You never knew what Nellie might do next. When they went shopping, she was forever running off somewhere. Though Ben was playing good parts and Kate was earning, money was still very short. A scrag end of mutton or a plump rabbit could be picked up for fourpence on the market stalls. With a bit of fat pork and a few onions and carrots, it would make a tasty meal for all of them. Having made her purchases, Sarah would look around for Nellie and the basket, but she was nowhere to be found. She had raced off to gaze longingly at the puppies, pushing her fingers through the wire netting, trying to touch the eager little black noses. She would be cuddling a kitten, or terrifying Sarah by feeding a horse squashed cabbage leaves. Goodness knows what will become of the child, her mother would think, brushing the dirty straw from her coat, tucking in the yellow curls, and tying the dangling bonnet strings firmly under her chin. She can't keep her mind on anything for two minutes together.

This particular day she was more worried than usual. Something had happened that could alter all their lives, that could disrupt the close-knit family ties that she had tried so hard to keep intact in the shifting life of the theatre. That summer at Edinburgh, Kate had played Arthur in *King John* and had given such a striking performance in the scene when the little prince is to have his eyes put out by order of his cruel uncle that there had not been a dry eye left in the theatre. Someone must have conveyed the news of this brilliant child actress to London, for a letter had come to Ben from Mr. Charles Kean, actor-manager of the Princess Theatre, inviting him to bring his daughter to the capital for an interview.

Of course Kate must go. Sarah knew that no actor could afford to miss an opportunity to become part of a great London management. But Ben had a long-term contract with the Liverpool Theatre. It meant the breakup of the family. She must take Kate to the city with George, who was too young to be left behind, and Benjamin, who had to be got to school somehow. At thirteen he needed the discipline badly. Ellen must stay to look after her father.

All day and far into the night, Ben and she discussed their problem, while Ellen listened and only half understood. The next few days saw a fury of packing. The big basket lined with American cloth and the old carpetbag were brought out. Food and necessities for the day-long journey were put together. Then Ellen and her father were at the railway station to see them off.

Ben put them into a compartment and dashed off to buy a magazine from the bookstall. Kate sat very prim in her best crinoline and velvet bonnet, looking down proudly at the black button boots and white stockings that were likely to be gray with smuts before the journey's end. Sarah was pouring last-minute instructions into Ellen's heedless ears. She must remember to cook her father's breakfast every day, watching carefully that the porridge wasn't lumpy. She must remind him to change his socks if he got his feet wet, be a good girl and do exactly as she was told. Ellen nodded and promised and didn't hear a single word. She was gazing enraptured at the engine, a huge black monster shining with brass and snorting smoke like a dragon while the stoker, an enormous, brawny figure, went on shoveling the coal from the tender so that showers of red sparks flew upward. The shriek when an engine let off steam, the smell of soot and sulfur, the bustle of travelers hurrying here, there, and everywhere, entranced her. All those hours and hours on the train racing through the countryside into the unknown: passionately she wished she too had been going.

The guard was already waving his green flag when Ben came panting back with a copy of *Household Words*. Mr. Dickens's new novel, *Bleak House*, was appearing in weekly installments. It was just the thing to wile away the hours in the railway train. He pushed it into Sarah's hands. The iron monster gave a great jolt and then seemed to leap forward with a chugging sound and they were off, waving and calling goodbye till Ellen could no longer see Benjamin's round head poked through the window and her mother's fluttering handkerchief.

It was to be more than a year before she saw her mother and Kate again—a time when her father "never ceased teaching me to be useful, alert and quick," she wrote long afterward in her diary. "Sometimes he hastened my perceptive powers with a slipper and always he corrected me if I pronounced any word in a slipshod fashion." But it was too a time when she ran wild, free of her mother's restraining influence and without the restrictions imposed on children in those strict Victorian days. She learned the value of independence. The theatre was her playground and it was also her school. There was no other training for an actor in those years except to be part of a company and pick up what you could from watching others.

In the greenroom where the players gathered when they were not rehearsing, Ellen would hear all the gossip of the day. Perched on some elderly actor's knee, the pretty child would listen to fascinating tales of the great players of the past. Edmund Kean, for instance, had only been dead since 1833, and a great many people still remembered him vividly. He had won his way to fame overnight, the dream of every half-starved actor in a mediocre provincial stock company.

It was on January 26, 1814, at the age of twenty-five, that Kean had set out from his miserable London lodgings to play Shylock at Drury Lane. He had had only one rehearsal and his fellow players bitterly resented this newcomer from the obscure provinces who for ten years had starved and clawed his way upward. He made his first entrance wearing black hair and beard, in defiance of the old tradition of the comic Jew with flaming red, greasy locks which was said to go back to Richard Burbage, the first Shylock in Elizabethan days. Within an hour he had made theatrical history. The half-empty theatre rocked with the cheering. He went on from triumph to triumph.

Samuel Taylor Coleridge, the poet, said that "seeing him act was like reading Shakespeare by flashes of lightning." And Charles Kean, in whose company Kate was now playing small parts, was his son. It made it all seem very close and real.

Then there was Sarah Siddons, who was so tremendous in

tragic roles that members of the audience had been known to faint or go into hysterics. Her niece, Fanny Kemble, was sweetly pretty, everyone said, but she couldn't be compared with her as an actress.

There was something else, too, that did not mean a great deal to Ellen then but would influence her future career. For two hundred years, ever since Charles II issued the first royal patent in 1660, only two theatres in London, Drury Lane and Covent Garden, were licensed to produce plays, the "legitimate" drama, as it was called. All the others had to make do with opera or musical plays or burlettas or vaudeville, but just four years before Ellen was born, this act had been repealed. Theatres began opening up all over the capital. "There will be splendid opportunities," said Ben, always optimistic.

England was growing richer. Industry was booming, even though up here in the north Ellen had seen the black mill towns in which factory workers lived huddled in tiny crowded houses without sanitation, without even running water. There had been lodgings where the bugs crept out of the walls at night, and even Sarah, brave though she was, had trembled at putting her children into the gray dingy beds alive with fleas.

But all these things were part of growing up and Ellen had a great deal of her father's vigorous, lively temperament. She enjoyed every moment as it came, and without her realizing it, the discipline and traditions and techniques of the theatre were soaking into her and becoming part of her very being.

In the end, Ben's cheerful optimism was justified. In the autumn of 1853 he received an invitation to join his daughter in Charles Kean's company at the Princess Theatre. He and Ellen traveled to London and there was a joyful reunion in the rooms Sarah had taken at the top of a tall house in Gower

Street, not too far from the theatre where they would spend so much of their time.

A small group of children were crowded together at the side of the stage, under the strict eye of Mr. Oscar Byrn, the dancing master. Auditions were being held for the part of Mamillius, the little son of Leontes in *The Winter's Tale.* There was none of the usual chattering and giggling. The opportunity to play a part in a production in which both Mr. and Mrs. Kean would be starring was too important to these youngsters born and bred in the theatre.

It was a chilly morning in March 1856, a month past Ellen's ninth birthday, and three years had gone by since she and her father had come to London. They still lived on the top floor in Gower Street, but now the family had increased to eight. There was Marion, whom they called Polly, just beginning to walk on fat, unsteady legs, and Floss, who was still in the cradle.

Outside the narrow limits of Gower Street and the theatre, there had been great events. England had gone to war with Russia. At Balaclava the gallant doomed charge of the Light Brigade had inspired the Poet Laureate to write his famous poem. In 1855 Tennyson's lines were on everyone's lips.

Their's not to make reply,
Their's not to reason why,
Their's but to do and die:
Into the valley of Death
  Rode the six hundred . . .

Ellen Terry at age eight COURTESY OF ROGER MANVELL

A thousand copies had been distributed to the troops besieging Sebastopol, and when the citadel fell at last, all London went mad with joy, cheering crowds raging up and down and bonfires burning at every street corner.

A young woman called Florence Nightingale had turned her back on fashionable society and struck a blow for women's independence by leading a band of brave companions to nurse the sick and wounded in the Crimea. Now it was over at last, and a Peace Conference had opened in Paris in February of this very year.

All these stirring happenings played little part in Ellen's life. There were other, far more pressing problems to be faced by the Terry family. Sarah, in a desperate attempt to increase their income, had accepted the position of wardrobe mistress and was glad of the extra money it brought them. Ben had been strongly opposed to it. She was an actress; it was not right, it was undignified. But Sarah had always been the practical one in their marriage. She had never had any illusions about her ability as a performer, and every day in the mirror she saw her good looks fading and her slender figure thickening. And so much was needed. Benjamin must have new boots for school; Kate, the rising child star, was badly in need of pretty dresses; Nellie, growing tall and leggy, was shooting right out of her sister's castoffs. Sarah was fiercely determined that George and Polly and Floss should have all the advantages denied to her three elder children.

Ellen's days had been divided between the theatre, where she ran wild backstage, and helping her mother to cook and clean and care for the babies. She knew only too well how welcome her salary of fifteen shillings a week would be if only she could win this part from the others.

One by one the children were called on the stage to speak their lines, with the stage manager playing all the other parts in a rapid undertone. Ellen, from her perch on the prompter's high stool, peered through a slit in the canvas. She could just see Mrs. Kean sitting in the stalls, a formidable figure, whaleboned and upright, a white handkerchief holding the looped brown plaits firmly in place, her nose jutting out like a beak, her stiff bombazine skirts spread majestically around her. Ellen regarded her with healthy fear and reluctant admiration.

"Miss Terry please," called the stage manager impatiently.

She started. It was Kate who was Miss Terry, she had always been just Nellie. Then she flung up her head and marched onto the stage, playing the scene for all it was worth, not even glancing at the script in her hand. It was one of the parts her father had made her learn long ago. She knew every word.

"That was very nice," said Mrs. Kean. "Thank you, my dear. That will do."

Halted in midstream, Ellen felt a huge wave of disappointment well up in her which threatened to break into tears. Fiercely she blinked back the tears. All that afternoon and evening in Gower Street she romped noisily with Benjamin, teased five-year-old George till he burst into sobs, and drove Kate to distraction snatching away the book from which she was trying to study her own part.

Early next morning when the postman hammered at the brass knocker that Sarah burnished to brilliance, she went down the four flights of stairs so fast they all held their breath, expecting disaster. A few seconds later she was back. On the landing she danced a hornpipe in sheer ecstasy, waving the script bound in shiny green American cloth above her head. Her first part, and a Shakespearean one! More lines than Kate, more even than her father. She was speechless with pride and pleasure.

Playtime was over, work had begun in earnest. She plunged into it joyfully, but it was only now that she began to learn how grueling the life of an actor could be. Charles Kean had none of his father's genius, though to Ellen's childish eyes he could appear very splendid. But he was conscientious, he worked hard at his profession, and with the invaluable help of his strong-minded, intelligent wife, his company was excellently run. There was no better training ground for a young actress.

When Edmund Kean first leaped dazzlingly to fame and fortune, he had raced home one night to hug his wife and toss his baby son in his arms. "You shall ride in a carriage, my love," he promised. "And Charley shall go to Eton!" He kept his promise, and the boy worshipped his father's memory despite the tempestuous life that broke up their home, the shocking scandals, the brandy that had wrecked his brilliant career. It was a lesson no man could afford to neglect. Charles Kean led a sober, decent, respectable life and expected his company to do likewise.

More of a schoolmaster than a player, he had a passion for historical research. He was the first actor-manager to set and costume a play in its correct period. Macready had attempted it, but never with such painstaking detail. His stage designer spent hours in the British Museum studying classical models for *The Winter's Tale*. Even the little go-cart Ellen dragged about the stage was copied from a child's toy painted on a Greek vase.

In days gone by, actors had dressed their parts in the clothes of their own time. Garrick had played Macbeth in a gold and scarlet uniform and white wig, and even Charles Kean could not prevent his wife from playing Hermione with layers and layers of starched petticoats under her flowing Greek gown.

Ellen might have giggled, except that Mrs. Kean played with too much fervor and passion to be a figure of fun. She never lost an opportunity of lecturing the children on clear enunciation. "A, E, I, O, U, my dears," she used to say, "are five distinct vowels, so don't mix them all up together as if you were making a pudding!" No one ever had a sharper tongue or a kinder heart than Mrs. Kean.

Rehearsals were long and exhausting, with no stop even for meals. The actors snatched something to eat when they could. If there was no play at night, they went on until four or five in the morning, Sundays included. Ellen would fall asleep in the middle of a sandwich, wake to play her scene for the hundredth time, and curl up again like a tired kitten on the window seat in the greenroom or in her father's arms or on a pile of old drapes and curtains in a corner of the stage.

The opening night came at last, on April 28, with Queen Victoria, Prince Albert, and the Princess Royal in the stage box. Wild with excitement, Ellen was being pulled into her pink tights by Mrs. Grieve, the dresser. "Peter Grieve-us," the children called her, but tonight nobody was laughing. Ellen could think of nothing but the nerve-racking thrill of playing her first part before such a distinguished audience.

In her red and silver dress, impetuous and overconfident, she made her first exit with such vigor that she tripped over the handle of the cart and fell flat on her back. An amused titter ran through the theatre. She fled from the stage broken-hearted, convinced that her career was doomed to finish before it had begun. She burst into frantic sobs, nothing would console her —till she was forced to learn the first hard lesson. Whatever happens, an actor must go on. Back she had to go to play another scene, and next day *The Times* called her "vivacious and precocious, a worthy relative to her sister, Kate."

Her father was pleased and even Mrs. Kean had a kind word. Elated, she went on to play the part until the theatre closed for the summer. And she came back in the autumn to another audition and to be chosen for Puck in *A Midsummer Night's Dream.*

It was a long part for a child of nine and her father coached her in it tirelessly. He would conduct extra rehearsals everywhere. Over meals, in the streets, in the horse bus—he even stood her on a shop counter and made her repeat her lines to the chemist! She enjoyed every moment of it, reveling in Puck's impish tricks and becoming quite unbearably cocky and conceited about her success, till the night she came up through the trap door to speak the final lines of the play and the stagehand let it swing shut too soon and broke her toe.

Kate, who was playing Titania, rushed to the rescue. She stamped her foot on the floor, but the man, mistaking the signal, only closed the shutter even more tightly. Nellie tugged and tugged, shaken with sobs. It was Mrs. Kean who got the shutter released at last, and spoke in a hissing whisper from the wings. "Finish the play, dear, and I'll double your salary!"

It was a wonderful inducement. Between agony and tears she got through somehow.

"*If we shadows have offended . . .*"
(*Oh, Katie, Katie!*)
"*Think but this and all is mended . . .*"
(*Oh, my poor toe!*)

And so on, right to the end. Her salary was raised to thirty shillings, a great advance, though she still got only sixpence a week pocket money. And the surgeon from St. Bartholomew's Hospital, who happened to be in the stalls, came around and set her toe.

She had learned the second lesson. An actor never gives in. While he is on the stage he belongs not to himself but to the play and to the audience. Pain, private grief, or personal anxieties must be left behind till the curtain falls.

Other parts followed. She walked on in *The Merchant of Venice* carrying a basket of doves, to the envy of the other children. She was "top angel" in the vision scene in *Henry VIII*, and as she swung high up near the ceiling in the flies, the heat from the gas lamps made her sick and dizzy at the dress rehearsal. She played Fleance in *Macbeth* and one night fell from top to bottom of the ladder offstage just as Mr. Kean started on his famous soliloquy. He was not pleased.

In the pantomine in which Kate played the White Cat, she had longed and longed to take the part of the wicked witch, Dragonetta, and was only reconciled to the insipid Fairy Goldenstar when she saw her costume. She was enormously proud of her first long dress, all in pink and gold, with a trembling star on the yellow hair, though it did mean tedious lessons in deportment from the dancing master.

Mr. Oscar Byrn was foppishly elegant. He minced about the stage in fancy waistcoats and elastic-sided boots. She had to walk with a blanket pinned around her waist and trailing six inches on the floor. The other children tripped and kicked like kangaroos, but she won high praise for moving with such exquisite grace. Then they had to "walk the plank" extending the whole width of the stage, quicker and quicker, until they could do the whole length without deviating an inch from the straight line.

"Eyes right! Chest out! Chin tucked in!" said Mr. Byrn in his high, piping voice, beating time with long, thin, beringed hands. The children giggled as they bowed and curtsied in the minuet, learning to dance with ease, dignity, and an upright carriage. Once learned, it is an art never lost.

There was other excitement backstage. One night, racing headlong back to her dressing room, she cannoned full into the white waistcoat of an elderly gentleman. Looking up with frantic apology, she saw with horror the majestic features of Mr. Macready. Would he fall into one of his famous rages? She waited, trembling, but the fine eyes under the jutting eyebrows were kindly. "Never mind! You're a very polite little girl and you act very earnestly and speak very nicely." She blinked at the unexpected praise. To her father it would mean far more than the newspaper critics. Overcome, she ran on, her imagination stirred by the air of grandeur that clung to the old actor.

Theatres are strange places. Out in front all is brilliance, color, and music, but backstage there can be gloom, crowded passages, dark small rooms, and moments of nightmare. The greenroom window looked out on a great square courtyard where the spare scenery was stacked. From her favorite perch on the window seat, Ellen would watch the rats swarming in gray hordes over the canvas flats. Once a storm broke and the thunder and lightning sent them scurrying hither and thither with high squeaking voices.

One night during *The Merchant of Venice*, she fell asleep in the deep recess and woke to hear a strange gabbling sound. Mr. Harvey, who played Launcelot Gobbo, the clown, was stretched on the sofa. "Nellie, little Nellie," he was gasping, his face twisted all sideways, his mouth working convulsively, froth on his lips. Stiff with terror, she could not move, and presently others came. A doctor was called and Mr. Harvey was carried away. It was a seizure, they said. She never saw him again.

"Let me not hold my tongue; let me not, Hubert:
Or Hubert, if you will, cut out my tongue,
So I may keep mine eyes: O spare mine eyes,
Though to no use but still to look on you . . ."

"No, no, no!" roared Mrs. Kean. "It won't do at all. Now start again and really try this time."

Ellen was rehearsing Arthur in *King John*, the part Kate had played so brilliantly six years before, and it seemed that she could do nothing right. Mr. John Ryder, a kindly man, who was playing Hubert de Burgh, smiled encouragingly and gave her the cue. Over and over again they played the scene until Ellen was so tired the words began to jumble together.

Mrs. Kean came sweeping up onto the stage, storming at her, telling her she was a stupid little girl who did not understand the first thing about acting and was too conceited and lazy to learn. She tried to stand up for herself, tried to say that she was doing her best, she really was, but it only sounded like insolence. Mrs. Kean lost all patience. She seized her by the shoulders, slapping her face hard. Shocked and mortified, Ellen felt the tears spring to her eyes, but her stern taskmistress gave her no rest. She had to go on through misery and gulps and aching throat.

"That's right, that's right. You've got it!" exclaimed Mrs. Kean. "Now remember what you did with your voice, reproduce it, remember everything and do it!" When the rehearsal was over, she gave Ellen a kiss and a pat on the shoulder. "You've done very well," she said kindly. "That's what I want. You're a very tired little girl. Now run home to bed."

Ellen never forgot the relief after so much misery. It marked the beginning of something new. On that day she became an actress. The parts she had played up till then had been no more than childish games. Now she began to understand that if she did not work she could not act. She started consciously to watch and listen, to see the play as a whole and herself as part of it. She was gripped by the wonder of it. She used to get up in the middle of the night, ignoring Kate's indignation, to try out new gestures in the mirror, speak her lines in different ways, make her voice go up and down in the right places.

Mr. Ryder helped. He was an excellent actor, a tall, heavily built man who reminded Ellen of an old tree that has been struck by lightning or a greenless, barren rock. He had played with Macready and told her how the great actor used to shake a ladder offstage, working himself up into a fierce rage for his entrance as Shylock. One day he spoke of his last, disastrous American tour, when he had been pelted on the New York stage with rotten eggs, potatoes, and worse. Ellen thought America sounded like a terrifying country. She listened in fearful fascination and wondered if she would ever go there.

All the wretchedness, the bitter tears, and the hard work had their reward. She was an outstanding success. The critics were enchanted. They spoke of her "great sweetness, clearness of enunciation, delicate light and shade and heart-touching pathos."

Night after night the audience thundered applause after their great scene, but Charles Kean had forbidden his actors to take curtain calls before the end of the play. John Ryder used to stamp up and down the greenroom in futile rage while out in front the people yelled for them. There was no love lost between him and his manager.

"Do ye suppose he engaged me for my powers as an actor?" he raged to Ellen one night. "Not a bit of it! He engaged me for me damned archaeological figure! Never you mind. When other people are rotting in their grave, ducky, you'll be up there!" And he made a sweeping gesture indicating dizzy heights of fame.

That was the year Kate played Cordelia in *King Lear*. She was only fourteen and all London raved about her. A critic wrote: "A peculiar dramatic sensitiveness and sensibility characterised the sisters Terry; their nervous organisation, their mental impressibility and vivaciousness, not less than their personal charms and attractions, may be said to have ordained and determined their success upon the stage." Kate and Ellen had well and truly arrived.

New horizons began to open out before them and changes had to come. Another little brother had replaced Floss in the cradle. The Terry family were bursting out of the narrow walls of Gower Street. With Ellen's increased salary they could afford to move to a house in Stanhope Street, Kentish Town, on the road to Highgate. From the attic window you could catch a glimpse of the wooded heights where Dick Whittington had heard the bells of London Town calling him back to fame and fortune.

It was a humble little house, but it was the first one they had ever owned. It had a pretty iron balcony overlooking the street, and a paved garden with doors opening onto it. Ellen and Kate spent happy hours with their mother rummaging through second-hand shops haggling over bargains, a little chest of drawers or a small table for the drawing room, in which Ben had installed a piano picked up for five pounds at an auction. For the first time they were able to entertain, even if only in a modest way, and they made new friends outside the limited world of the theatre.

Charles Reade was a great kindly bear of a man more than six feet tall, a playwright and critic, passionately attached to good causes; his novel, *It's Never Too Late to Mend,* had furiously attacked prison abuses. He could not have been a greater contrast to his friend Tom Taylor, who might have been the very embodiment of Mr. Dickens's Pickwick. He was small, plump, untidy, absent-minded. His eyeglasses, forever slipping down his nose, were tied up with string. In the evening he would change into the velvet coat, knee breeches, and buckled shoes of an earlier age. But he too was a journalist, dramatic critic on *The Times,* and had collaborated with Reade in a very successful play called *Masks and Faces.*

Both these distinguished scholarly men were ardent theatregoers and they took the Terry girls under their wing. At their fine houses they met for the first time all the intellectual society of the day, the poets, the painters, the writers. To Kate, self-contained and confident of her own ability, it meant little except to introduce her to influential people who could help her career. To Ellen, far more sensitive, hungry for knowledge, her young mind groping after the education she had missed in her childhood, it was a revelation.

At Tom Taylor's home in Lavender Sweep overlooking the chestnuts and green grass of Clapham Common, there were evenings of music and poetry when, entranced, Ellen listened to readings from *Morte d'Arthur* or the *Idylls of the King*, Tennyson's rich rhythms bringing into vivid life Arthur and the Knights of the Round Table, poems which had inspired the paintings of the Pre-Raphaelites, Millais, Rossetti, Holman Hunt, and a tall, dark-bearded, shy man called George Frederick Watts, who came very rarely.

There were invitations to grand society houses. To the end of her life, Ellen remembered a Christmas party at Half Moon Street where she and Kate danced with the Duke of Cambridge, cousin to Queen Victoria, their fair hair newly washed and shining, wearing the white muslin frocks Sarah had made for them, working far into the night with a single candle, determined that her girls should look as fine as the rest of the aristocratic company.

All this came to a temporary finish in the summer of 1860. The Keans, whose splendid productions had been steadily losing money, decided to cut their losses. They gave up their lease of the Princess Theatre and sailed for America. The Terrys were thrown back on their own resources, a challenge that Ben had already planned to meet in his own way.

2
Growing Up

THE ROYAL COLOSSEUM in Regents Park was a favorite place of entertainment, and the strange, imitation-stalactite caverns beneath the main building were one of its chief attractions. In this eerie, gloomy spot Ellen used to hide herself away from everyone. She was studying the part of Juliet on her father's advice, thrilling with passion and terror in the Potion scene.

"*O look! Methinks I see my cousin's ghost*
Seeking out Romeo, that did spit his body
Upon a rapier's point. Stay, Tybalt, stay!
Romeo, I come! This do I drink to thee."

She would fall headlong to the stone floor while the walls dripped and ghosts seemed to start from every shadow. It was all very dramatic and enjoyable and in vivid contrast to the "Drawing Room Entertainment" with which they were amusing the large audiences upstairs every night.

While they were still playing at the Princess Theatre, Ben had rented the tiny playhouse in Ryde, on the Isle of Wight, during the summer recess. The Isle had become highly fashionable as a holiday resort ever since Queen Victoria had built Osborne House and spent so much time there with her husband and children.

Ryde, just across the Solent from Portsmouth, was home ground to Ben. He knew it intimately. He put on a program of light entertainment, farces and sketches exploiting the talents of his two clever daughters in comic parts made famous in London which they and the audiences thoroughly enjoyed. It was hard work, but it was holiday too. They lived in Rose Cottage, loaned to them by Aunt Lizzie, their mother's sister, and in between rehearsals they joined Sarah on the beach, romping with the babies growing brown and healthy in the sunshine.

Sometimes they dipped up and down in the surf, shrieking when the waves broke over them as they clung to the wheels of the bathing machine. Then they would clamber inside to pull off their frilled and flounced bathing dresses, the wooden floor gritty with sand under their bare feet, and all round them the clean salt smell of the sea.

At other times they would all pile into one of the carriages and drive the five miles around the island, with Ben whipping up the pony in fine style, or spend an afternoon wandering over Carisbrooke Castle, where the unhappy Charles I had been imprisoned the year before his execution.

The success of these summer seasons had given Ben encouragement to carry out his present plan. He had inherited a little money at his mother's death. He found two short plays in which all the parts could be acted by Kate, Ellen, and himself, with a young pianist, Sidney Naylor, who would also serve as musician.

Ellen would come racing up from the cool caverns, late as usual, her mind echoing with Juliet's tragic lines. She would pull on checked pants, stick a jaunty cap on one side of the yellow curls, and stroll on as a saucy, fly-by-night, cigar-smoking schoolboy in *Home for the Holidays,* with Kate playing the sweet young miss, his sister, and then pretending to be a starchy, prim old maid. It was all great fun. Their youth, their verve, and Ellen's sense of comedy as she played the buffoon, loving every moment of it, carried them through and won all hearts. The "Entertainment" was a roaring success.

At night after it was all over, they would link arms, Nellie with their father and Kate with their mother, and tramp back across the park, through the dark alleys with dim yellow lamplight, to Stanhope Street, with Ben inventing a dozen amusing games to make the long walk seem shorter for the two weary young girls.

They could afford help in the house now. A woman came in daily to scrub and to wash the sheets and table linen on Mondays. There was a housekeeper to leave in charge when they went on tour, which Ben planned to do just as soon as they had fulfilled their London engagements.

Sarah had not wanted to go away and leave the home she loved so dearly and had fought so hard to win. It meant a split in the family once more. Benjamin was twenty-one, just the age to give anxiety with his wild unsuitable friends. There was George at school, and Marion, Floss, and baby

Charles. But who else could look after the girls? They were not children any longer. They needed to be protected from overenthusiastic admirers. There were their clothes to be washed and mended and pressed. They had to be persuaded to sleep for an hour in the afternoons before the evening performance while she and Ben and young Naylor set up the stage in the small halls in which they played. There were her own parts to be studied and dressed. It was back to the strolling days, even though they did have a few more comforts.

To Ellen, just thirteen, the months of touring were pure enchantment. With the happy heedlessness of childhood, she saw it all as a glorious adventure: the new audiences they captivated every night, the old inns they stayed in, warm and cozy, with a fox mask snarling at them from the mantelpiece or a gigantic brown fish with glazed eyes staring at them from its glass case, and always the smoldering peat fires on the hearth. Above all, there was the rich, beautiful countryside with the blossoming hedgerows and the smell of grass and summer flowers.

It bred in her a deep and abiding love which she was never to lose all her life through. Usually they traveled by carriage. Railways had not penetrated everywhere in the West Country, and once, when money was short, they walked from Bristol to Exeter, a distance of more than seventy miles.

She saw summer dawns and the sunsets she had almost forgotten in the fog and smoke and grime of London. She saw the gray and gold cathedral at Wells with its moat, where the swans come sailing under the stone walls of the Bishop's Palace, tugging at the bellrope when they are hungry, and by ancient custom are instantly fed.

She stood under the great ruined arches of Glastonbury,

where legend says Joseph of Arimathea brought the Holy Grail after the Last Supper and where in the Middle Ages the monks miraculously came upon the grave of Arthur and saw for a magical moment the long-dead king with the golden-haired Guinevere lying beside him. Fragments of what she had heard so recently in the drawing room at Lavender Sweep came flashing back into her mind.

So all day long the noise of battle roll'd
Among the mountains by the winter sea;
Until King Arthur's table, man by man,
Had fallen in Lyonnesse about their Lord . . .

It was so exquisitely sad the tears would start to her eyes. The very next moment she would be shrieking with laughter at some joke shared only with her father, as he chased her across the grass. She would fall headlong, skirts flying up, so that Sarah would frown and Kate would stamp her foot with annoyance. Why couldn't Nellie behave properly?

On Exmoor there were the deer racing across the skyline like a lovely frieze, and shaggy brown ponies running free with a shy grace. "What are you thinking of, Nellie?" someone asked her as they drove along.

"Only that I would like to run wild in a wood forever," she answered gaily.

Her mother said nothing, but she felt the familiar disquieting pang of anxiety. If only Nellie were not so unpredictable, so unlike the others, so easily swept away by her eager enthusiasms.

On Sundays, still loyal to the faith in which she had grown up, Sarah would take her two pretty daughters to church or chapel with her handsome husband beside her. Neat, decent, respectable, they were not at all like the "pomping" folk, as the old country people called the flashy, disreputable strolling players, of whom they heartily disapproved.

This carefree life came to an end in 1861 when Kate was offered a season at the St. James's Theatre. Back they went to London, and Ellen's name was entered for the first time in a theatrical agent's book.

Madame Albina de Rhona, a Frenchwoman who had danced her way successfully from Paris to St. Petersburg and then to London, had ventured into management at the tiny Royalty Theatre in Soho. On a windy morning in October, Ellen set out for an audition, borrowing Kate's new pink silk bonnet trimmed with black lace, to give herself courage. Madame was small, dark, and vivacious. Ellen had never seen anyone like her before. Her knees shook and her voice went up into a squeak out of sheer nerves, but she got the part, and at the first rehearsal she was nearly driven out of her wits.

The tiny Frenchwoman danced around her in an absolute frenzy, shrieking at her half in English, half in French. She was so small, with such an exquisite figure, her every movement so precise, that Ellen at fourteen felt all gangling arms and legs. Her hands seemed to get in the way, they were so large. Desperately she tried to hide them, tucking them under her armpits.

"Take them down!" screamed madame. "Mon Dieu! It is like an ugly young *poulet* going to roost!"

She had a difficult scene to play in a melodrama from a novel by Eugène Sue set in Jamaica. A servant who bore a grudge against the rich planter's family sets a live snake on the innocent young daughter which winds itself around her throat and slowly strangles her. At the rehearsal Ellen screamed and screamed till she was hoarse, but madame only shook her head, storming and raving, and at last like a small wild cat she came tearing up onto the stage, shaking Ellen till she was so breathless and terrified that she broke into hysterical, heart-rending cries.

"*Voilà!*" exclaimed madame triumphantly. "That is it. *C'est magnifique!*"

On the first night she was a sensation. The audience applauded madly, Madame Albina kissed her and called her a genius. It was all very gratifying.

She went on to play five other parts in as many weeks and, cramming the lines into her overburdened memory, had her first experience of stage fright, that nerve-shaking, terrifying sensation that comes to all actors at least once, when the words fly out of the head, the throat dries up, the knees turn to jelly, and an icy-cold fear creeps up the spine. There is nothing to be done but go off, seize the book from the prompter, and read the part—which is what Ellen did. If madame boxed her ears for it, it just could not be helped.

Years afterward in her diary Ellen tried to distill what she had learned from these early experiences. "Imagination, industry and intelligence," she wrote. "They are all indispensable to the actress but of these the greatest is without any doubt imagination."

It was a quality that was growing in her, expanding her vision, extending her understanding. It created in her a longing for new ideas, new experiences, new knowledge. That February she was fifteen. The season at the Royalty came to an abrupt end. She and Sarah went to join Ben and Kate at the Theatre Royal in Bristol, where she was to meet someone who was to change the course of her life.

Bristol had been built on the banks of the Avon. The ships that came up the river from the sea seemed to sail into the very heart of the city. Queen Square, where Ben had taken rooms for his family, was surrounded on three sides by a forest of tall masts. When Ellen walked to the theatre in King Street, the air was filled with the smell of tar, spices, tobacco, and leather being unloaded from the docks. The sails of the graceful tea clippers were like the white wings of sea birds.

In the Llandoger Trow, the ancient, half-timbered inn by the harbor, seafaring men still gathered in the dark-paneled taproom. On this very spot the Cabots, father and son, had planned their famous voyages in search of the Northwest Passage, discovering Newfoundland and the far north of Canada.

Mr. J. H. Chute, who had married Macready's half sister, had gathered an excellent company for his season of modern and classical plays, in which Kate would be the leading lady. Ellen's parts would range from Nerissa to her sister's Portia in *The Merchant of Venice* to Cupid in a gay burlesque called *Endymion*. An actress in a stock company, she discovered, had to be able to turn her hand to anything. She must act, sing, or dance just as she was commanded. It was that or out you went! It was a disconcerting but very useful experience.

In no time, stage-struck young men were handing up bouquets of country flowers and sending around little presents.

They waited hopefully outside the dark narrow stage door to see the Terry sisters come out. The presents were all sent back at once and the girls were never alone. Ben or Sarah always accompanied them. A flashing smile, a murmured word of thanks, were all they permitted their admirers.

One night they had a visitor who was bolder, who did not wait outside but was ushered in by Mr. Chute himself, who asked if the two charming Miss Terrys would consent to join in a reading of *Midsummer Night's Dream* at his house in Portland Square, where the Bristol Shakespearean Society held their meetings.

Ben would have agreed at once, but Sarah laid a restraining hand on his arm. She was not sure of this Mr. Edward William Godwin. He came of an old Bristol family; he was an architect and eminently respectable; but he was young, only twenty-eight; he was elegantly handsome, with brown eyes and an irresolute chin hidden by the silky beard. There was something about him which she instantly distrusted. He was too artistic, he spoke with too much freedom. She would have much preferred the invitation to have come from his wife. However, as he explained to them, Mrs. Godwin suffered from delicate health and rarely went out. He usually came alone to the theatre.

Ellen, entranced by the charming voice, the sweet smile, waited breathlessly for her mother's consent. It came a little reluctantly. Kate and she could go together.

Kate thought the house in Portland Square strange and bare. She had never seen anything like it before. She wrinkled her nose disdainfully at the cream walls, the shining wood floors with the fine Persian rugs, the blue and white porcelain from China, the exquisite Japanese prints, the antique furniture.

The Godwins must be very poor, she thought, to have everything so very plain. Ellen fell in love with it at first sight. She wandered from one beautiful object to another, touching them with wonder, asking questions, wanting to know about everything.

Godwin, whom many people regarded as aloof and unapproachable, was amused by this lovely, eager child with her corn-colored hair and eyes blue as a summer sea. He told her how his friends, the sea captains, brought him rugs from Bokhara and Samarkand. He told her about the Japanese artist, Hokusai, who died in 1849 and whose fame had spread throughout Europe. He showed her his designs for the Town Hall at Northampton which he had entered in a competition and which had triumphantly won. It had made his name as an architect. He had built it in the style of the Italian Renaissance and he read to her from the book that had been his inspiration, *The Stones of Venice*. John Ruskin, he said, preached that art was part of life; paintings were not just objects to hang on walls but an expression of the human spirit.

Ellen did not know what the Italian Renaissance was. She had scarcely heard of Ruskin or the aesthetic movement. She did not realize that the young architect was one of the leaders in the revolt against the ugly, cluttered, overdecorated houses and furniture which the Industrial Revolution and the newly rich merchants and tradesmen had made fashionable. She only knew that something in her responded instantly, that this was the beauty she had been seeking and now at last she had found it. The first invitation was followed by others. The two girls became frequent and welcome visitors at Portland Square, sometimes with other guests, sometimes on their own to take tea with Godwin and his wife.

One day, when they had been talking about the theatre, he asked them if it thrilled them to be playing on the very boards where Garrick had once acted with Peg Woffington, where Edmund Kean had played, and Mrs. Siddons with her brother, John Philip Kemble. He told Ellen that he had seen her as Puck in London, and he criticized the Cupid she was playing now.

Irritated at his manner, Kate said, "It's absurd to take a burlesque so seriously. You are as bad as the critic who tears us to pieces every week in the local paper."

Godwin smiled. "I don't agree with you. Even a burlesque can be beautiful."

Something about his look of amusement convinced Ellen that he himself was the author of the clever articles which she had carefully cut out and pasted into her scrapbook. It gave him an added glamour in her eyes.

Kate thought him affected, with his passionate devotion to beauty and his taste for history, which had led him to trace his own ancestry back to Earl Godwin, father of Harold, the last of the Saxon Kings, once lord of Bristol, who had been defeated and killed by William the Conqueror at the battle of Hastings.

Ellen thought it romantic. She would listen rapt while he talked of Shakespeare and poetry or played Bach to her on the organ he had installed in the hall of his house. At Queen Square she spoke so much about him that Sarah's anxiety redoubled, especially when, wild with delight, she told her mother that he had promised to design the dress she would wear as Titania when Mr. Chute opened the theatre in Bath with *Midsummer Night's Dream.*

Together they made the dress at Portland Square. He showed

her how in ancient Greece the material for a woman's dress was damped, then bound up and tied so that, when it dried, it was all crinkled and clinging like crepe. It was the first lovely dress she had ever owned and she wept bitterly when the management would not permit her to wear it.

Sarah was thankful. It was not at all proper. It showed every line of the slender young figure. Thank goodness the season was almost over and they would all be going back to Stanhope Street. She hoped fervently that she had seen the last of Mr. Edward Godwin.

"Head up, back straight, now sink to the floor gracefully, not bobbing up and down like a serving wench in a tavern, but gently like a swan, with your gown falling round you like plumage." Mr. Chippendale was teaching Ellen to drop a sweeping curtsy in the grand manner such as was practiced when *The Rivals* was first produced in the eighteenth century. Mr. Chippendale was so old he might well have sat on the stage of Drury Lane and watched Sheridan himself rehearsing his plays, thought Ellen rebelliously, hearing him click his tongue impatiently when she hit the floor with a bump instead of coming to rest with the grace and lightness of a bird.

"Again," he said. "Come along now, try again."

She gritted her teeth and went on doggedly until he pronounced himself satisfied. She knew she was not making a success of the part of Julia, try as she would. She had come back from Bristol feeling restless and discontented with her life. In Stanhope Street all had been fuss and upheaval. Little Tom had been born in a hurry, very nearly in the middle of dinner one day. She was having to shoulder a great deal of the work of the house, since Kate was playing leading parts opposite the great Fechter at the Lyceum and could not be expected to do so much as pick up a duster. They seemed to have forgotten that she was plunged, alone, into a new season at the Haymarket.

They were a company of distinguished veterans trained in the old school. Their bows, their curtsies, their grand manner, the indefinable style which they brought to their work were something to see, but she was in no mood to appreciate it. They were all so old and they treated her as if she were a raw, inexperienced, awkward child, criticizing her every word and movement. She resented it furiously.

On the very first night of *The Rivals,* she had brought the play to a finish with a light, lilting, unconventional gaiety in her last speech, and the idiot of a prompter had stared at her open-mouthed, waiting for her to go on, instead of bringing down the curtain. There was a very awkward pause and Mr. Buckstone, the manager, went into a rage. He scolded her severely in front of the whole company. She stood sullenly, hating him and hating, too, Mr. Edward Askew Sothern, the star of the company, a light comedian who had made a tremendous success in America and was unbearably conceited about it. Every time he played opposite her, he tormented her, pulling her hair, giving her sly pinches, trying to make her forget her lines, teasing and making fun of her.

Always before, she had been cushioned and protected by her parents and her elder sister. At Bristol she had been petted and spoiled. Now she was having to fight for her very life in the harsh, unkind, rough-and-tumble of a theatrical company of which she was the youngest and most insignificant member.

With the idealism and intolerance of youth, she detested the idle gossip in the greenroom, the backbiting, the malice which tore every reputation to shreds. One day she swept out in a huff, dropping the curtsy she had practiced to perfection and boldly speaking the line from another Sheridan play: "I am called away by particular business but I leave my reputation behind me." Her audacity earned her more black looks.

The only enjoyable times were the Sundays she and Kate spent with the Taylors at Lavender Sweep, playing croquet under the chestnuts, listening to Clara Schumann play her husband's sonatas on the piano, or Robert Browning read his dramatic lyrics. He was so handsome and so sad. He had just returned from Italy after his wife's death. Everyone knew about his famous elopement with the invalid Miss Barrett fifteen years before. Sometimes he read the poems he had written for her.

Escape me?
Never—
Beloved!
While I am I, and you are you,
So long as the world contains us both . . .

Tom Taylor was arranging for Kate to be painted by his friend George Frederick Watts, but there were difficulties. She could not go to his studio alone—it was simply not done. Sarah had her hands full with the new baby and the care of the younger children, so Ellen must accompany her sister. One afternoon they took the horse bus as far as Hyde Park Corner and then walked the two miles through the lanes and fields to Little Holland House.

THE TATE GALLERY

George Frederick Watts around the time of his marriage to Ellen Terry, a self-portrait

Ellen looked at it curiously as they picked their way through the farmland. It was an old, rambling place on Lord Holland's estate. Cromwell had once walked in these gardens with his son-in-law, Colonel Ireton, in the days of the Civil War. Now it was occupied by a Mrs. Thoby Prinsep, whose husband was a wealthy member of the India Office.

She welcomed Kate effusively, taking both her hands in hers. "I am so glad to see you, my dear. Now you must feel quite at home and learn to call me and my sisters by our Christian names. We have no formality here."

The two girls were overwhelmed by the three handsomely dressed middle-aged women who greeted them in the drawing room. They were glad to be conducted through the narrow passages, up steps and down again, to the studio where Mr. Watts, whom everyone affectionately called "Signor," was waiting for them.

Watts was a shy, delicate man with dreamy eyes, dark curly hair and beard, and a diffident manner. Ellen had seen him before at Charles Reade's parties, before she went to Bristol. While he fussed about getting Kate seated on the dais, moving her head this way and that and arranging the canvas on his easel, she wandered around the studio looking at the paintings.

Outside the long windows there was a lime avenue, there were green lawns shaved to velvet, and roses clambering over stone walls. It reminded her of Godwin's house. It was like a paradise where only beautiful things were permitted to enter. It did not occur to her to wonder how it was that a man of forty-seven could be content to live out his life in someone else's house, the pampered protégé of three rich, art-loving ladies.

She asked him a question and he turned around, really seeing her for the first time. The sun coming through the windows changed to gold the harvest-colored hair. He was supposed to be painting the girl on the dais, but this was the face he wanted. From a gawky child she had become lovely, with something mysterious, something medieval and mystic, about her. In his mind's eye he saw her at once as a St. Joan, a warrior saint, an Ophelia, a young girl reaching out to pluck a flower as if she were reaching out for life. He suggested that she should come and join her sister and he would paint them together.

Ellen was surprised. It was Kate who was beautiful, everyone said so; she was the ugly duckling. She went obediently to do as he asked, leaning her head on her sister's shoulder. Swiftly the artist sketched in the fine brow, the strong nose and wide, generous mouth. It was the inspiration he had been seeking all his life.

All during that summer they went to sittings at the studio. Sometimes there were garden parties at Little Holland House under the sweet-scented lime trees. The Prinsep ladies were known among their intimates as "Beauty," "Dash," and "Talent." They welcomed writers, artists, and distinguished political figures. Ellen met William Ewart Gladstone, the son of a Liverpool merchant who had made his fortune in the slave trade. He was Chancellor of the Exchequer under Lord Palmerston, and a prominent member of the Liberal Party. She thought he was like a sleeping volcano. She looked into the piercing dark eyes and seemed to catch a glimpse of the red-hot crater beneath the crust.

Disraeli, soon to be Tory Prime Minister, fascinated her. He made her think of Shylock with his hooked nose, his oiled black curls, the flashy rings on his fingers, and his fancy waist-

COURTESY OF THE HON. MRS. HERVEY BATHURST

THE SISTERS *by G. F. Watts*

coats. She had read some of his novels: *Venetia,* with its picture of Lord Byron, which she had to hide from her mother; and *Tancred,* which described a family of strolling players even closer to life than Dickens's Vincent Crummles in *Nicholas Nickleby.*

Watts had finished painting the picture, which he called "The Sisters," and had begun to make lightning sketches of Ellen. She loved to be in the studio with him, spending hours posing for him, cleaning his brushes, playing the piano to amuse him, or just sitting close beside him as he worked. Life at the Haymarket seemed sordid and ugly in comparison. She thought she would like to stay beside him in this beautiful house forever.

When one day he took her in his arms and kissed her, she was in a daze of happiness. She was sure she was in love. She would be his inspiration and she longed to spend her life making this great artist happy. She would be everything he wished.

Neither of them really knew the other. Watts wanted to take this lovely innocent child away from the dangers and temptations of the theatre. He wanted to guide and educate her. He consulted the Prinsep ladies, on whom he depended for his living, and they agreed with him. They saw her as an ideal young wife for their favored artist, someone whom they could control and dominate.

To Ellen it all seemed like a wonderful dream. On a freezing morning in January 1864, just a month before her seventeenth birthday, she got up very early and helped her mother to bathe her little brothers and sisters. Then she put on the brown silk dress that Holman Hunt, the artist, had designed for his friend's bride, and picked up the quilted white satin bonnet with its sprig of orange blossom. Her father was waiting for her in the hall. He put an Indian cashmere shawl around her shoulders before they stepped into the brougham that would take them to St. Barnabas Church in Kensington.

Sarah watched her coming up the aisle and was glad that her difficult, wayward Nellie was safely settled at last. Now she could turn her mind to the other children. Only Ben was unhappy. He had hoped to see his Duchess a great actress one day, achieving the fame he had somehow missed himself, and now all his ambitions for her had come to nothing.

When Ellen drove away after the reception in her little sealskin cap and jacket with its coral buttons, she looked back at her parents with Kate and the children, her throat aching, tears not very far away.

Her new husband said affectionately, "Don't cry. It makes your nose swell."

She blinked back the tears, smiling at him, putting a trembling hand in his, certain that she was entering into a paradise of happiness.

Ten months later she was back at Stanhope Street, bewildered, wretchedly unhappy, her marriage broken and lawyers arranging a separation, when she did not even understand where she had failed. She was not yet eighteen and it seemed to her in utter despair that her life was finished.

3

Interlude

ELLEN LOOKED AROUND the small, crowded room which Sarah had furnished for her at Stanhope Street, and ungratefully hated everything in it, the wallpaper with its ugly cabbage roses, the ball fringe on the velvet looped along the mantelpiece, the cheap Nottingham lace curtains at the window. There was none of the spaciousness, none of the beauty that had surrounded her at Little Holland House. Outside, the smoke and soot of London depressed her after the clean sweet country air.

She picked up another woolen stocking from the huge pile on her lap. However did the children make such enormous holes in their heels, she thought impatiently. She stabbed at them with her darning needle to the rhythm of Kate thumping out Beethoven's "Moonlight Sonata" on the piano downstairs.

For the hundredth time she went over the last year in her mind. What had gone wrong with her marriage? "Incompatibility of temper," the deed of separation said, but it had not been like that, not at first. She and Signor had been ideally happy. She had posed for him gladly for hours and hours, lying along a willow branch as "Ophelia," posing in her wedding dress against a bank of dark camellia foliage for "Choosing," standing in heavy armor for "Sir Galahad" until she had fainted with fatigue.

Very soon after her marriage they had visited Tennyson at his house in Freshwater in the Isle of Wight. Mrs. Prinsep had been angry with her because she had run out into the garden to play games with the poet's two sons, Hallam and Lionel, instead of sitting demurely by her husband's side in the drawing room, but dear Mr. Tennyson had not minded at all. He had smiled at her when she slid quietly into the room to listen to him reading his poetry. He had taken her walking in the fields, telling her the names of the wild flowers, plucking the scarlet pimpernel for her, teaching her how to recognize birds by the peculiarities of their flight. It had been hot in the sunshine and she still had the brown straw hat like a mushroom that she had tied on over her flowing hair.

She smiled a little to herself because that had been another silly thing that had upset Mrs. Prinsep. She had told her that she looked like a schoolgirl and ordered her to put up her hair, and one afternoon, bored to death with the dull company in the drawing room, she had pulled out all the pins and let it tumble down around her shoulders just for a lark. It was a childish thing to do, but need they have attacked her so cruelly? She had been accused of vulgarity, of shaming her husband, of insulting his friends. Publicly rebuked and upbraided, she had

THE ROYAL PHOTOGRAPHIC SOCIETY OF GREAT BRITAIN

Ellen Terry at sixteen, a few days after her marriage to Watts. Photographed by Mrs. Julia Margaret Cameron in Tennyson's home on the Isle of Wight

felt the hot Terry temper flare. There had been an unpleasant scene.

Then one afternoon an old acquaintance had called. Repressed, snubbed into silence, made to feel inferior and of no account, shut in her room when they expected famous guests, Ellen had welcomed Edward Godwin with unrestrained pleasure, proud to show that she too had a distinguished friend. Signor had liked him at once. They shared some of the same ideas about art and poetry and Shakespeare. When they were all three in the studio together, they had been happy, both the men enjoying her high spirits, amused at her mistakes, telling her she was learning fast. Soon, they said, laughing at her antics, she would know as much about sculpture and painting as they did.

Sometimes when she visited the family at Stanhope Street she would come home by way of Marylebone, where Godwin had his office, with rooms above. After all, she was married now. She did not need a chaperon any longer.

His delicate wife had died since the days at Bristol. He was working hard and she found that he was lonely too. He enjoyed her visits, showing her the designs he was submitting for the building of the new Law Courts. He asked her opinion, he made her feel that she was someone of value, not a badly behaved child.

One day when she called she found him suffering from a bad cold, coughing and feverish. Accustomed to caring for the children when they were sick, she stayed longer than usual, making him hot drinks, cooking food, and persuading him to eat it. She was quite unprepared for the storm that broke above her head when she returned to Little Holland House.

Mrs. Prinsep and her sisters accused her of unspeakable

things. She was shocked and deeply distressed. She turned to her husband for support and understanding and found none. He went from the room, leaving her to face the tempest alone. After that, it had been nothing but pain and wretchedness until they bundled her home like a piece of merchandise that has been found faulty.

Well, it was no good brooding over it. She got up and put away the workbasket, staring at herself in the mirror. Her face looked white as a ghost's and she had grown so thin her dresses could have wrapped twice around her. She felt like Mariana in the moated grange.

She only said, "My life is dreary
He cometh not," she said;
She said, "I am aweary, aweary,
I would that I were dead."

She had written that in a letter to a friend that very morning. But now she had to go down and be pleasant to their visitor. The Reverend Charles Lutwidge Dodgson rather fancied himself as an amateur photographer. He was coming to take pictures of them all outside in the garden. He had known Ellen since her childhood and had just published a book under the name of Lewis Carroll. *Alice in Wonderland* had been almost the only thing to draw laughter from her in these last dreary months, though sometimes she felt just like poor Alice, drowning in the flood of her own tears with the Mouse and the Duck and the Dodo, all the strange creatures that she had met down the rabbit hole.

It was two years before Ellen returned to the stage, and then only at her father's urging. To his great distress, Kate, at twenty-

Studies of the Terry family by Lewis Carroll

ARNOLD ROOD COLLECTION

Ellen and her sister Florence

The Terry family: seated at either side are Ben and Sarah; Ellen, in dark dress, is standing in the doorway next to Kate, in white

three one of London's most successful young actresses, with a brilliant future before her, was giving it all up to be married. She took her farewell as Juliet, the tears pouring down her face when she appeared before the curtain for the last time, with a gold bracelet clasped around her wrist inscribed with the names of a hundred plays and the words "To Kate Terry on her retirement from the stage from him for whom she leaves it."

Sarah was delighted. Arthur Lewis was everything a careful mother could want for her daughter. He was the son of a wealthy linen draper, and partner in a prosperous business. He was handsome and rich, with charming manners. Kate would have servants and a fine house in Campden Hill only a stone's throw from Little Holland House. Everything a young woman could desire would be hers for the asking. Ellen did not envy her any of these things, but she did think it must be wonderful to have someone like Arthur who loved you deeply for yourself alone.

These last years had not been easy for her. She had been made to feel unwanted, a burden on the household. She found herself becoming irritable with the children she adored, because they kept asking questions. Even little Fred, born a year after Tom, had his ears boxed one day, though she was hugging him the next minute. Kate had been resentful because Arthur's mother had been bitterly opposed to her son marrying an actress, and the scandal of Ellen's separation did not help to make things easier.

But it was not all wretchedness. Some friends, taking pity on her, took her to France as companion to their own daughter. The Paris of Louis Napoleon's second empire was in its last blaze of glory. She fell under the spell of its elegance, its luxury, its air of nonchalant gaiety. She saw the Empress Eugénie in her white and silver crinoline leaning back in her carriage like an exquisite waxwork. In the Bois de Boulogne the orchestras were playing Offenbach's lilting melodies, the young officers waltzed at the masked balls till dawn and flocked into the Opéra entranced by the daring cancan dancers in *La Vie Parisienne.*

Baron Haussmann's wide, straight boulevards seemed wonderfully clean and quiet after the noisy clatter of London's narrow, grimy streets. She drank coffee at Tortoni's, tried to smoke a cigarette and choked over it, went to the Easter Mass at the Madeleine and fainted with ecstasy when the Host was raised, and thrilled at Sarah Bernhardt, only a year or two older than herself, making a striking debut at the Comédie Française.

Back in London, she found Stanhope Street more a prison than ever. There was no pleasure in returning to the stage, though the Queen's in Long Acre was a fine new theatre and Arthur Wigan was a veteran actor-manager who had worked with Charles Kean and Macready. The plays were trivial, the parts she was playing bored her, she seemed to be suffering from a perpetual bad cold, and she was furious when they billed her as Mrs. Watts instead of using the name that had been hers from childhood. She was badly in need of sympathy and understanding and the only person who gave it to her was Edward Godwin.

Sometimes she met him at his office, sometimes they went walking together in Regents Park. She listened to him as she had done at Bristol and in her need for kindness and friendship never once realized that he talked exclusively about himself. But she was not a child any longer and he too was lonely and frustrated in his work. Almost without knowing it, they were falling more and more deeply in love, and she dare not tell her mother of these meetings, knowing how greatly Sarah would disapprove.

Toward the end of the year, she was to play Katharina in *The Taming of the Shrew*. On a foggy, cold morning in December she went down to rehearsal to meet her Petruchio, a young man of twenty-eight who called himself Henry Irving though he had been born Johnny Brodribb. She knew something about him. He had made some sort of small success in London in a play called *Hunted Down*. Opinions were divided about him. John Lawrence Toole, the little comedian of the company, who was his friend, said that one day he would be right at the top of the profession. Other people dismissed him as hopeless. "Can't talk, can't walk, and a voice like a rusty saw. No spark, you know, m'dear," was one comment.

She looked at him curiously. He was tall, with raven black hair falling over his forehead. He was stiff with self-consciousness, awkward in his movements. He played Petruchio as a brigand chieftain instead of a lighthearted Italian gallant. Yet there was something about him, a kind of imprisoned power struggling to free itself. For ten years he had forced his way upward from nothing. He had worked day and night, he thought of nothing else, he would go without food to buy himself a book he needed or a stage jewel that might help him to play his part.

Such devotion to his art, such an indomitable will to succeed, seemed strange and almost frightening to her. She never stopped to wonder what he thought of her, but she did remember how aloof and reserved he was, how nervously sensitive to ridicule, how he never joined in greenroom gossip, and above all there was his quiet, grave courtesy. When she came racing up to the queue waiting outside the office on pay days, late as usual and always in haste to get away, he would immediately give up his place to her.

Once outside the theatre and hurrying to meet Godwin, she

would forget him instantly. Secretly between them they were coming to a decision, the most momentous she had faced in her life, and she could think of nothing else.

In October 1868, when she was twenty-one, she came out of the theatre one Saturday evening, walked quickly down Long Acre, met Godwin on the corner, and went away with him, leaving the stage behind her as she thought forever.

The cottage was called "The Red House." The bay windows in the two rooms downstairs looked out on a great stretch of Gusterd Wood Common. There was a kitchen and an old bake-house at the back. Upstairs there were two bedrooms and a tiny landing. The walls were painted a pale primrose and the furniture, designed by Godwin himself, was slender and black. Ellen loved it.

It was December of 1869. They had been together for more than a year of unclouded happiness, with only one painful incident.

Her flight had caused her parents alarm and distress. A few weeks after she had disappeared, the police had summoned them to identify the body of a slim young girl with golden hair, washed up from the Thames. Knowing how unhappy she had been, they thought a tragic suicide only too possible. The tears blurring his eyes, Ben had recognized the pathetic figure as his daughter, but Sarah, nerving herself to closer examination, remembered the strawberry mark on Nellie's arm and knew they were mistaken.

When Edward brought the news back to their Hertfordshire retreat, she had flown up to London to show them she was still alive. Despite their joy, it had been an uncomfortable meeting. Shocked and upset, they implored her to return home.

Ellen knew that she had broken the strict code of Victorian morals. Watts would never consent to divorce her, he dreaded scandal far too much, so it was not possible for Edward to marry her. If she continued to live with him, Sarah told her more in sorrow than in anger, she must cut herself off from the children, from Kate, from all decent society. She left as soon as she could. She had made her choice. Edward Godwin needed her as no one else had done, and to him she would give all her love and devotion.

She did not regret leaving the theatre. She had always loved the country. Now she learned to know it intimately. Of course she made mistakes. She had never had to feed two hundred chickens and ducks before, or milk a goat or harness a pony, and Edward was far too busy to do any of these things. She plunged into her new life with zest.

She planted vegetables and flowers in the garden, watching them hopefully, and horribly disappointed when they did not always grow. She cleaned and scrubbed and studied Mrs. Beeton on cookery instead of a Shakespearean part. She was teaching herself to prepare all kinds of delicious meals, sometimes with disastrous results.

The chickens had all been given names. Duke, Lord Tom, Noddy, Lady Teazle, and so on, strutted up and down the yard. It had been a hard struggle to decide which was to have its neck wrung. When she brought it, crisp and golden, to the table, Edward looked at it doubtfully.

"Hasn't this chicken rather an odd smell?"

"How can you?" she replied indignantly. "It must be fresh. It's Sultan."

But of course he was right. They burst into laughter as it struck them both at the same moment. She had quite forgotten to remove Sultan's insides! That day they ate vegetables covered with bread sauce and pastry made light as a feather, a skill she had learned from her mother and never forgotten.

She had a mania for scrubbing everything. The floors were spotless, the furniture shone with beeswax and hard rubbing. She even washed the hair of her little maid-of-all-work and Essie complained to her mother, who came bustling up from the village protesting volubly. "Never washed 'er 'ead in me life!" she exclaimed emphatically. "Never washed any of me children's 'eads, and just look at their splendid 'air!"

The snow had come early that winter and when she went out in the garden the two fir trees stood like black sentinels on a white carpet etched against a pale sky. They looked like one of the Japanese drawings Edward loved so much. She fed the chickens and the ducks, made sure the goat was safely housed in the shed with plenty of straw, and went back into the house with the bulldog she had to protect her during Edward's frequent absences snuffling and snorting at her heels.

Of course Edward could not always be there. She knew that. Sometimes he would work at the table in the sitting room for days at a time and in the afternoons they would go rambling over the common and down the lanes, coming home with branches of dog roses and armfuls of harebells and white marguerites from the fields. But then he had to go up to London to see clients or to lecture or spend evenings with his friends—one in particular.

James McNeill Whistler was born in Lowell, Massachusetts, and spent his childhood in St. Petersburg, where his father, a military engineer, had built a railway for Tsar Nicholas I.

After his education in Paris, Whistler had come to London in 1859. He was a friend of Rossetti, Millais, and Holman Hunt, but his paintings were nothing at all like those of the Pre-Raphaelites. He shared with Edward a passionate love of everything Japanese, which had been the rage in Paris. He loved the clean cool lines, the abstract formality of their paintings. His "Little White Girl" in the Royal Academy had stirred up a storm of criticism. It was like flinging a pot of paint in the public's face, Ruskin had said scornfully. When he and Edward got talking about their beliefs and ideals, they were likely to forget all about time and catching last trains.

During the summer it had been fun to take the pony trap and drive across the common through the village of Mackery End and the little town of Wheathampstead, along the lovely banks of the river Lea and into Hatfield Station, to meet him. They would drive back in the scented summer evening and after supper he would read to her the poems of Robert Herrick or Blake's *Songs of Innocence*, which she was discovering for the first time, or from Charles Darwin's *The Origin of Species*, a new book which shocked her just as it had outraged all England.

"Are we all descended from monkeys? Then what about Adam and Eve and the Garden of Eden?" she would ask.

Godwin laughed at her, calling her an old-fashioned Tory and quoting Disraeli's dry comment in a speech at Oxford. "The question is this. Is man an ape or an angel? I am on the side of the angels."

He told her one day, "You should have no room for small thoughts. Thought should be great."

"How can I make my thoughts great?" she asked him. "What must I do?"

"For a whole night you must lie out in the fields alone and watch the sky from dusk to dawn."

Obediently she did as he said. She looked up into the mystery of the night, and the stillness, awe, and beauty sank into her, became part of her. Only in the early morning did she creep back into her room to sleep, and the memory of it stayed with her all her life.

But on this December night for the first time she felt lonely and depressed. The baby she was expecting was due any time now and she had hoped so much that Edward would be here with her. Yesterday she had driven the pony trap through the slushy snowy lanes and waited and waited on the icy platform, watching every train come in until the last one had gone through and all hope had vanished.

The six-mile drive through the dark winter night had seemed very long, and as she was crossing the common, a drunken farm laborer had climbed up beside her, trying to seize the reins. She could smell his whisky-laden breath. Panic-stricken, she had summoned all her strength to beat him off with the handle of her whip. She shivered at the memory.

She piled more wood on the fire and with Essie's help dragged the big mattress down from the bedroom into the warm sitting room. She had seen too many of her little brothers and sisters come into the world not to know the signs. She sent the maid to fetch Dr. Rumball, who had been looking after her, and lay down on the mattress, trying to stifle her fear by reading *The Watching of the Falcon*, a new book by William Morris, another of Edward's Pre-Raphaelite friends. It helped her to get through the time of waiting.

The doctor arrived in good time, bringing his kindly wife with him to help the young mother through her labor. Ellen adored her daughter as soon as she was put into her arms, a

COURTESY OF ROGER MANVELL

William Godwin around the time of his involvement with Ellen Terry

solemn, dark-eyed baby with a strong will of her own and a mop of brown hair. They had already decided on a name. She should be called Edith after Eadgyth, daughter of Earl Godwin, wife to Edward the Confessor and sister of King Harold, whom Edward liked to think of as one of his ancestors.

The fact that Edward came back dispirited because a client for whom he had been designing a house had taken offense at his architect's firm refusal to change his ideals of what was right and beautiful was all forgotten in their joy at their first-born.

Besides, as soon as she was up and about again, she was going to learn how to trace his drawings and designs for him. If she worked hard every evening, she could not only save him a great deal of expense but earn an extra guinea or two to help with the housekeeping.

Edy was just over two years old when Teddy was born, on January 16, 1872, a fat round baby with hair so fair it was almost white. Ellen, cradling him in her arms, thought how happy Edward would be. He had always wanted a son, and he needed something to cheer him. Things had not gone so well with them during the last two years.

It was just that he had so much to worry him, she said to herself loyally, but sometimes they had come near to quarreling. The last time she had seen him, when she was struggling to harness the pony, ready to drive him to the station, he had caught sight of her pulling at the heavy straps and had suddenly exploded into unreasonable anger. "Haven't you cost me enough already without obliging me to fetch a doctor to you?"

It had been hard to keep back a sharp answer. But she had

learned to know him by now. He hated trouble. He avoided facing up to things. If she or Edy were ill, he would discover he had urgent business elsewhere, leaving her to cope alone.

There had been one moment in the past when she felt she could not go on. He had been away for days and days and had sent no word. She had sat up night after night copying the elaborate architectural drawings for him by lamplight until her eyes were sore and inflamed, and she had gone to meet him at the station tired and anxious, hoping against hope that this time he would come. When she left the empty platform, she wondered wearily if it ever occurred to him how cruelly disappointing it was and how long the evenings were with only a fretful child for company.

It had been raining. The air was heavy with moisture and the trees dripped on the shawl she had wrapped around her head and shoulders. On the way home through the woods, nervously starting at every sound, the lantern on the cart casting tall shadows before her, she saw something shining in front of her. She stopped and took the lantern to investigate.

The brilliant eyes of a large frog stared at her, and beyond him there was another and another. The warm rain had brought them out of the ponds. They swarmed over the path wherever she looked. To drive forward or back seemed impossible. In her agitation she dropped the lantern and it went out. In total darkness she groped her way back to the cart. There was nothing to be done but wait, shivering, for the cold dawn. Then, when it came at last, there was still the journey home and the pony to be unharnessed and fed before she could think of herself.

She got him into the stable, rubbed him down, and watered him. Then she reached into the rack above to pull down the hay into his manger and a mouse fell straight down her back. The shock nearly sent her into wild hysteria. It was the end of everything. She couldn't stand it another moment. She would take Edy and run away, anywhere so long as there was safety, light, and company.

But of course she didn't. She had too much courage and resilience. The very next day she was laughing at herself. Fancy being frightened of a mouse!

A week or so later, when the huntsmen in their pink coats came charging across the common surrounding the cottage, the madly baying dogs sending the chickens and ducks into a frenzy and the Master demanding to search the bakehouse, she outfaced him with an act of outraged indignation that would have done justice to Mrs. Siddons. When they rode away and all was quiet again, she opened the bakehouse door and let out the fox.

Sometimes she did not know what she would have done without Mrs. Rumball. The doctor had died shortly after Edy's birth, but his widow was a constant visitor. "Boo," Edy called her, the nearest she could get to Rumball, and Boo she remained to everyone.

Money was desperately short. Edward depended on the fees of clients and they had been very few and far between. He had begun to design furniture and wallpaper but his ideas were too modern, too far in advance of the public taste to be popular. He accused her of extravagance, but it was not easy to keep house on two pounds a week. When he came home tired and irritable after a frustrating day in London, he grumbled at the simple supper of eggs, cheese, and salad from the garden and and she hesitated to tell him that the butcher would not supply more meat till the bill was paid, that she was forced to bake her own bread and run across the common at night to beg milk from the farm now that Fred was no longer there to bring an extra pint to her in the morning.

Fred Archer had been a firm friend for the first year. Thirteen years old and thin as a herring, he was crazy about horses and consumed with a burning ambition to be a jockey like his father. Now he was apprenticed in Newmarket and she missed his cheery, cocky face and his confident belief that the first time he rode a winner, his Miss Nellie could bet her last shilling on him and he'd make her fortune.

Kate had just had her second baby, surrounded with every luxury, with her mother hovering over her and a loving husband anxious that she should want for nothing. Now and then Ellen thought wistfully how wonderful it must be to live like Kate without a single worry. Edward had no more head for money than she had. When he had money, they spent it freely with no thought for the future. But she did try to be careful. She had not had a new dress for years. She sewed the little smocks for Edy herself and went to church in a plain blue and white cotton gown while Essie went in silk.

"I don't 'arf like it, Mum," she used to say. "They'll take you for the cook and me for the lady."

But now she had her darling baby, and when Edward came back from London, he was in the highest of spirits, bringing her a tiny monkey as a present, overjoyed to see his son, proud of the fact that his design for Leicester Town Hall had won first prize in the competition. He was full of plans to build a new house for Ellen and his growing family on a site he had already seen, only a few miles away, at Fallows Green, near the village of Harpenden.

He brought another piece of news too. Casually one evening he remarked that Henry Irving had made an outstanding success in a melodrama called *The Bells.* It was an adaptation from a French play, he told her, recently played in Paris by the famous French actor Coquelin. Everyone thought Irving crazy, daring to match himself with such a great player, but he had done it in spite of them. Now all theatrical London was pouring into the Lyceum to see his extraordinary study of a murderer driven by his conscience to a terrible death.

She listened with interest. Was it possible? Had that strange repressed young man's genius broken free from its chains at last? For a moment the old life flared up in all its fascination and she had a momentary hunger for the glamour of the footlights, the thrill of a first night. Then it was all forgotten in the excitement of planning their new house.

Long afterward Ellen was to remember the summer that followed as one of the happiest in her life. They built the house and it was beautiful, with an enormously high pitched roof, a huge studio, a nursery for the children, and a handsome roofed gate. They spent so much money on it and the new furniture that there was none left over to pay the trades people, but what did that matter?

James Whistler came to visit them, bringing Ellen a set of Venetian glasses and a dinner service of exquisite blue and white china which exactly went with the Japanese drawings and the wallpaper Edward had designed with a motif of sunflowers and birds in flight.

Despite the fact that there was very little money to spare, they decided on a holiday in France, taking Edy with them and leaving baby Teddy in the charge of Boo.

They went to Bayeux in Normandy first, where Edward

wanted to study the famous tapestry, then on to the Gothic Cathedral at Lisieux, to Nantes and to Rouen, where Joan of Arc had been burned to death in the marketplace.

High up in the tower of the cathedral one morning, with Edward talking of pointed arches, lancet windows, and flying buttresses, Ellen heard the choir practicing and one boy's voice, pure, effortless, rising like a lark into the blue sky. It was an unforgettable moment of magic, and when they climbed down the winding stone steps, there at the bottom was Edy, her little face rapt.

"Shh, Mama! Miss Edy has seen the angels."

Edward laughed and swung her up into his arms as they went out happily into the sunshine.

Once they were home again, the unpaid bills caught up with them. They were beset with difficulties. Edward was in London endeavoring to mortgage the house and raise a loan. Ellen at Fallows End was desperately trying to fend off bailiffs, one of whom had established himself in the hall of the house.

Then something extraordinary happened. She was driving home one day when in a narrow lane a wheel came off the pony cart. She got down and was standing beside it wondering what on earth to do when the hunt came leaping across the hedge and one of the huntsmen, a tall man mounted on a fine horse, stopped and came back.

He raised his top hat politely. "Can I do anything to help?"

They stared at one another in astonishment. He exclaimed, "Good God! It's Nellie! Where have you been all these years?"

Unbelievably, it was her old friend, Charles Reade.

"I have been having a very happy time," she answered quickly.

"Well, you've had it long enough. Come back to the stage!"

"No, never!"

"You're a fool," he went on. "You ought to come back."

Across her mind flashed the picture of the bailiff sitting in the hall, immovable as a rock. She said half laughing, "Well, perhaps I would think of it if someone would give me forty pounds a week."

"Done!" said Charles Reade. "I'll give you that and more if you'll come and play Philippa Chester in my play, *The Wandering Heir.*"

He went on to explain that the actress playing it had to leave to take up another engagement, that it was doing well and he did not want to take the play off. It was a lovely part, he assured her, just like Rosalind in *As You Like It,* and exactly suited to her.

Ellen was scarcely listening. She was thinking of forty pounds a week. It would make all the difference to their lives. It would pay their debts. It would help Edward so that he could go on working at what he wanted to do and forget his difficult clients. Why, in a few weeks she could earn enough to keep them for a whole year. It would be back to the happy days at the beginning. It was a wonderful opportunity. All she wanted to do was race home, tell Edward about it, and persuade him to agree.

And so, by the merest chance, and thinking no further than the next step, she made the second great decision of her life, one that was to lead her back to the theatre, to awaken in her something which had lain sleeping for six years, and to bring her to undreamed-of heights of fame and popularity.

4

Lady of Belmont

HOW STRANGE IT SEEMED to be back in the noise and clatter of London after the deep quiet of the country. In the morning Ellen would hurry from the house they had taken in Taviton Street to the theatre in Long Acre, running all the way through Soho if she were late, because she did not want to waste money on a cab.

It was a busy quarter. Brown-skinned onion-sellers from Spain, pie men with trays of steaming pastry, Italians with their glowing braziers of roasting chestnuts, flower girls, children with penny bunches of home-grown cress, jostled one another in the gutters, all crying their goods as they had done for centuries.

The streets were crowded with carriages of every kind,

broughams, landaus, victorias, hansoms, and the four-wheelers everyone called "growlers" from the habitual surly temper of the drivers, all reeking of horse sweat and the stable. In the evening when she came home she would meet the lamplighter lighting the yellow gas lamps one after the other, reaching up with his long pole with the protected light at the tip.

She was thankful that she had been able to leave Edy and Teddy at Fallows End in the care of Boo. The thick London fogs, yellow and choking, were not good for children. Finding her way back into the old life at the Queen's Theatre turned the days into one hectic rush. The childhood training in technique stood her in good stead, but six years out of the theatre is a long time and she had to work hard to justify Charles Reade's faith in her.

On the first night she was sick with terror, knees like jelly, hands shaking, feeling her breath give out and her strength fail through sheer nervous exhaustion, but she need not have worried. She had not been forgotten. The audience warmed to her. The critics were smiling and jotting down excited comments on their programs.

From his place at the side of the stage, Charles Reade watched and noted the hundred different places where she was at fault. She needed more pace, she lacked variety, her speeches wanted more bite . . . and yet how lovely she was. Nose rather too long, mouth nothing in particular, hair the color of tow, yet she was beautiful. Her expression killed any other pretty face you saw beside her, he thought. Her figure was too lean and bony, her hands too large, yet she was a pattern of fawn-like grace. She was an enigma, never the same for two minutes together. The eager child he remembered had grown into a disturbing and fascinating woman.

She was still cut off from her family and Charles Reade took the place her father had once held in her life. He praised her, bullied her, coaxed her, picked on all her mistakes, giving endless advice, watching her night after night and sending around little notes.

"Pace is the soul of comedy," he reminded her, and another day, "You have vigour but you turn limp. You have limp lines, limp business. The swift rush of words, the personal rush should carry you off the stage. It is in reality as easy as shelling peas if you will only go by the right method instead of by the wrong."

But she was not a child any longer. The years of love and happiness and suffering away from the theatre had matured her, deepening her understanding. She knew what she wanted. They would argue furiously over how a line should be spoken or a scene played. Sometimes they quarreled violently—this lovely young actress of twenty-seven and the elderly dramatist and author—only to have the fun of making up: going out to lunch together to celebrate, or buying each other little presents. She had thought she never wanted to act again and now found herself thrilled, excited, working immensely hard and loving every moment of it.

"Dear, kind, unjust, generous, cautious, impulsive, passionate, gentle Charles Reade," she wrote in her diary. "A stupid old dear and wise as Solomon!"

Tom Taylor had come back into her life too. He praised and criticized from his seat in the stalls and invited her to the Sunday parties at Lavender Sweep.

The Wandering Heir was followed by an adaptation of *It's Never Too Late to Mend.* Immersed in rehearsals by day and acting at night, Ellen struggled to furnish the house in Taviton Street in the style that Edward liked, bringing up some of their favorite pieces from Fallows End. There was straw-colored matting on the floors, white walls, curtains of a delicate gray-blue Japanese design, and fragile wickerwork furniture.

The years they had spent together, the books and pictures they had studied, had influenced her deeply. The fashionable women that she was now meeting daily had abandoned the crinoline. They were tightly laced into whalebone corsets; their elaborate skirts, trimmed with yards of ribbon or ruches of velvet, were drawn back over enormous pads of horsehair and gathered into a bustle. Ellen's dresses, designed by Edward, had the simple flowing lines of a medieval gown. On anyone else they might have looked absurd. On her they acquired the grace and beauty of a Pre-Raphaelite painting.

It was not always easy to keep the balance between the theatre and home. She had always tended to throw herself into whatever was interesting her to the exclusion of everything else, and unfortunately Charles Reade and Edward had taken an instant dislike to each other.

Edward began to resent her absorption in the theatre and the people she met there. A young actor of twenty-one named Johnston Forbes-Robertson, who was taking over a part in the play, was sent by Reade one day to call on her. An artist as well as an actor, he fell in love with the house and with Ellen. She laughed at his adoration but he came more and more often. He painted her portrait. He visited them at Fallows End when they escaped for a few days in the country to see the children.

Edward was being forced to realize that the girl who had slaved and scrubbed and cooked for him was a person in her own right. She not only was earning far more than he was, keeping both him and the babies, but was lovely and desirable in the eyes of other men. He took to spending more and more time with his artist friends at the Arts Club.

He refused to accompany her when Tom Taylor took her to the first night of *Hamlet* at the Lyceum on October 31, 1874. It was an event that all theatrical London was eagerly anticipating. She knew that Henry Irving was acting under the management of Colonel Hezekiah Linthicum Bateman, a tall, handsome man, who had been born in Baltimore and, having failed as an actor, had become a theatrical manager. She was intensely curious to see again that nervous, edgy, moody young man she remembered so well. He had by all accounts played some notable parts since his success in *The Bells*. Now he was submitting himself to the greatest test of all. Hamlet is a part in which an actor must win or lose all. If he succeeds, he can become enshrined among the immortals, but if he fails, he will be condemned forever to the ranks of the mediocre.

From the first moment the performance left her stunned. It was new, revolutionary. It was unlike any other *Hamlet* she had ever seen. She was breathless with admiration, enthralled and exalted. Gone were all the black plumes, the sable trappings of woe, the false pompous monotonous ranting of the earlier tragedians. Instead she saw a young Prince, grave, dignified, dressed in simple black only relieved by the gold chain around his neck and the icy glitter of his silver-hilted sword proclaiming the aristocrat and the soldier. The tight-fitting sleeves of his doublet were turned back with white cuffs showing off his sensitive and expressive hands.

This was indeed, as Ophelia lamented,

The expectancy and rose of the fair state,
The glass of fashion and the mould of form,
The observed of all observers . . .

THE NATIONAL PORTRAIT GALLERY

Ellen as painted by Forbes-Robertson, 1876

For Ellen it was a revelation, the perfect Hamlet. For the rest of her life she held to her opinion that it was the finest part he ever played. That night in her diary she tried to find words that conveyed the essential qualities—strength, delicacy, and distinction. There were no theatrical touches, no false moments. He made no attempt to go out to the audience but instead he drew them to him, so that when the curtain fell after five hours of intense concentration, they responded with tremendous acclamation.

The critics as always were divided. One said Irving was "simply hideous . . . a monster"; another found only the scenery worthy of comment; but a third wrote that the performance was "beyond all praise. The town will go down on its marrowbones to Hamlet the Dane." And he was right. Irving's striking success brought Shakespeare back into several other theatres on a wave of popularity.

"Here a little child I stand,
Heaving up my either hand . . ."

"Cold as paddocks," prompted Ellen. She looked fondly at Edy. In the tiny kimono given her by James Whistler, with her dark hair cut in a fringe on her forehead, she looked as Japanese as the wallpaper. Ellen was determined that her children should speak beautifully, so she was trying to train them early, just as her father had done with her and Kate.

At six years old, Edy was very serious and eager to learn, not like Teddy. Plump and rosy-cheeked, he mumbled the words after his sister, his eyes fixed longingly on his breakfast egg.

"Cold as paddocks though they be,
Here I lift them up to Thee,
For a benison to fall
On our meat, and on us all."

"What are paddocks, Mama?" asked Edy.

"It's an old country word for toads or frogs, darling, and Robert Herrick was a country clergyman."

Across the table, Edward frowned impatiently behind *The Times*. It was so difficult to teach the children when he did nothing at all to help. He got up and abruptly left the table before they had finished, going out of the room without a word. The front door slammed behind him.

Boo came to fetch the children for their morning walk. Almost without noticing it, she had slipped into the position of companion and close friend. Teddy as usual made a fuss, kicking at the table leg and pouting. He hated walking.

"Lazybones!" said his mother, and kissed him because in his tiny white suit, with his fair hair and gray eyes, he looked so adorable and so like Edward. But when they had gone, she went upstairs to finish dressing, staring at herself in the mirror.

She was painfully thin. Her dress, cut long and straight like a medieval tabard, was of deep yellow woolen material. Her "frog" dress, Edy called it, because it was speckled with brown like the back of a frog. It had always been part of her temperament to be up or down, to be gloriously happy or very miserable, and at the moment, with no stage work in prospect, harassed by debts, afraid for the children's future, she felt utterly wretched and as if there were no hope anywhere.

What had happened between her and Edward when they had once been so marvelously happy? He had been angry with her because she had gone off on tour. But after Charles Reade's season at the Queen's had come to an end and he had asked her to remain with the company, what else could she have done? She could not desert him after his generosity and kindness, quite apart from the plain fact that they needed the twenty-five pounds a week that he would pay her. She knew Edward hated to be alone. Without her gaiety and encouragement he became depressed, and the children got on his nerves, distracting him from his work. She had been torn between the two loyalties but, after all, it was only for a few weeks.

She smiled for a moment. There had been some mad merry pranks with Charles Reade. There had been his play *Rachael the Reaper* with a country farm setting. He had developed a sudden passion for realism. Never would she forget the day when he arrived at the theatre in a four-wheeler with a collection of little pigs, a large dog, and a very cross-tempered goat from a circus. While Charles Kelly, who was playing the farm laborer in the play, was trying to pacify the angry goat, the pigs all escaped, scampering off in all directions.

"That's a relief at any rate," exclaimed Kelly, watching poor Charles Reade frantically chasing after the piglets. "I shan't have those damned pigs to spoil my acting as well as the damned dog and the damned goat!"

On the first night the dog bit Kelly's ankles and in anger he kicked the animal by mistake into the orchestra's drum!

Rachael, the goat, spent the summer browsing on the lawn of Charles Reade's house at Knightsbridge, with everything a goat could desire, and still she grew thinner and thinner. Then one night when they were all in the drawing room with the windows open and someone playing the piano, in pranced Rachael, lively and quite at home. All this time she had been pining for the bright lights and the sawdust of the ring, so back she went to the circus and thus ended the experiment in realism!

There was not very much fun in Ellen's life at the moment. It had been a shock to come back after tiring weeks of traveling around the provinces to find they were so deeply in debt that the brokers' men were sitting in the kitchen at Taviton Street and nearly all the furniture in the house had been carried away to pay their bills. Edward had fled to the Isle of Wight, leaving instructions that nothing was to be sent after him. She had to cope with the situation as best she could.

While she was away, he had become involved in writing articles about the place of women in architecture, for a magazine concerned with women's rights. The emancipation of women, their right to take up a career in professions hitherto considered sacred to men, was one of the burning questions of the day. Accustomed to earning her own living since childhood, Ellen was inclined to be impatient of all such frantic causes and she did not care for the young girl assistant he had taken into his office to support his theories. Ellen was the least jealous of women, but Beatrice Phillips at eighteen, daughter of a sculptor, was altogether too adoring, too worshipping. Edward had become her hero. She listened to him spellbound, just as Ellen had once done.

The sound of the doorbell roused her from her gloomy thoughts. She ran down the stairs to answer it.

"May I came in?"

The elegant figure with the silvery voice, dressed in fashionable Parisian black, followed her into a room that had been stripped of everything except the Japanese matting on the floor and an almost life-size figure of the Venus de Milo with a little tripod in front of it, from which rose long curls of blue incense.

The visitor wrinkled her pretty nose and put up one hand to shield her eyes. "Dear me," she remarked humorously, and smiled.

Ellen had known Mrs. Bancroft at the Theatre Royal in Bristol when she was still Marie Wilton. Now with her husband, Squire Bancroft, she was running a brilliant and successful season of domestic drama by Tom Robertson at the Prince of Wales Theatre. She was an accomplished actress of polished modern comedy. She gave a quick, amused glance at the statue and then at the bare room before she turned to the tall young woman in the quite extraordinary dress. She came straight to the point. She and her husband were intending to revive *The Merchant of Venice* and they would be glad if Ellen would play Portia for them.

Portia! A part she had studied, a play she loved and knew intimately. It seemed too good to be true.

"Well, what do you say?" went on Mrs. Bancroft a little impatiently. "Will you put your shoulder to the wheel with us? We have been thinking of asking Mr. Godwin to design the settings and costumes for us."

Ellen could not believe her own ears. She answered joyfully, incoherently, that of all things, she had been longing to play a Shakespearean part again, that she and Edward had made a close study of Venice in the grand days of the Doges, that all this last year he had been working on a series of essays on the architecture and costumes of Shakespeare's plays.

She was so excited and happy that she hardly knew what she said, except that she agreed to play for twenty pounds a week. She would have taken half the money rather than let the chance slip from her, and after all, Edward would be earning too, so they would be rich again.

It is said that after the publication of *Childe Harold* Byron woke one morning and found himself famous. Ellen had a similar experience when she played Portia. The critics were ecstatic in praise of her. "The very poetry of action," wrote one. "The bold innocence, the lively wit and quick intelligence, the grace and elegance of manner and all the youth and freshness of this exquisite creation," wrote another.

On one man in the audience her performance made an unforgettable impression. Henry Irving found it difficult to recognize the irresponsible, careless, unpunctual girl he remembered. The beauty and detail of the Venetian settings were stored in his retentive mind for future use, but the Shylock he thought quite abominable. One day he would show the British public how the Jew ought to be played. But Portia was a different matter.

In Belmont there is a lady richly left,
And she is fair . . .

says Bassanio to his friend Antonio. From her first appearance, jesting with Nerissa about her suitors, in blue and white brocade, a deep red rose at her breast, Ellen captivated her audience. In the casket scene she wore a dress the color of almond blossom, the golden head rising regally out of the delicate lace ruff. But it was in the trial scene that she impressed Irving most. Like some slender young man in her black lawyer's gown, she charmed him with the utter naturalness of her manner, the compassion of the "mercy" speech, the gentle humor and gaiety, her swift lovely movements, the faultless enunciation that her father had taught her long ago. No other actress he had ever seen possessed this indefinable star quality that no audience can resist.

"Is your name Shylock"?
Merchant of Venice
Ellen Terry.

ARNOLD ROOD COLLECTION

Ellen as Portia. The inscription is in her handwriting

In her diary Ellen was to write: "Never until I appeared as Portia had I experienced that awe-struck feeling which comes, I suppose, to no actress more than once in a lifetime—the feeling of the conqueror . . . elation, triumph, being lifted on high by a single stroke of the mighty wing of glory—call it by any name, think of it as you like—it was as Portia that I had my first and last sense of it."

It was a triumph not won without effort or pain. Only a few weeks before the opening night Edward Godwin walked out of the house, abandoning her and his children. Afterward Ellen would never willingly speak of that time of wretchedness even to her most intimate friends.

Why had he gone? The thought tormented her. There could be so many reasons. Jealousy perhaps, because she was forging ahead in her profession, leaving him far behind. She had developed an independent mind of her own. Yet they were both temperamental artists. They had clashed before, but only to make it up again as lovers will. Maybe now he felt unjustly that she put the children before his interests. In a last attempt to assert himself, he threatened to take them from her. Edy screamed in terror and Teddy, not understanding, ran to hide in a cupboard. Ellen rounded on him, fierce as a lioness defending her cubs. Bitter, angry words were spoken, cruel and hurting, between two who had loved so dearly, and then the door slammed and he was gone, never to return.

The success of *The Merchant of Venice*, the appreciation of the artists and poets who had flocked to see Edward's work and came again because of her, the letters she received from adoring young men, all helped a little, but the wound took a long time to heal.

The house at Fallows End was sold and she moved to lodgings in Camden Town, high up on the hill, where the air was fresher for the children and there was a big garden they could play in. It was a tiring journey by horse bus to and from the theatre, but she did not dare spend money too recklessly since there was no one else to help provide for them.

A few months after he left her, Edward married Beatrice Phillips, his assistant. This hit Ellen cruelly. It was the end of the old life and the start of a new one, but it was hard to endure and she had to face it quite alone.

"You *did* look long and thin in your gray dress," said Edy accusingly. "When you fainted I thought you was going to fall into the orchestra—you was so *long*."

The little girl had been to see her mother act for the first time and at eight years of age was already very critical.

Ellen smiled across her dark head at the tall man who had called to take her to the theatre. "Edy is so severe with me that if I listen to her any longer I shall give up the stage in despair," she said laughingly.

It was nearly two years since *The Merchant of Venice*. She had only played a few more parts at the Prince of Wales Theatre. Her success had been a little too remarkable for Mrs. Bancroft to swallow. Now she had an engagement with John Hare at the Royal Court Theatre and had met an old friend in the company.

Charles Kelly had shared in the fun of the pigs and the goat and had played with her in *The Wandering Heir*. He was as unlike an actor as anyone could be. His real name was Wardell and he had been a soldier in the 66th regiment, fighting all through the Crimean War. His father was a clergyman in Northumberland and had been a close friend of the great novelist, Sir Walter Scott.

Charles was such a handsome bulldog of a man, thought Ellen. He had taken Teddy on his knee, showing him his watch and trying to teach him to tell time, but the little boy was obstinate, as usual. Yet Charles was patient with him. He was not at all like Edward had been, or like any of the artistic, aesthetic young men, such as Forbes-Robertson for instance or the red-haired poet Swinburne or Edward Burne-Jones, the artist, who crowded around the stage door and wrote her languishing love letters. She liked Kelly because he was simple and straightforward. True, he was not a brilliant actor, but in the right part he could be both charming and effective and he was so good with the children.

She was worried about Teddy. He was lazy and self-willed. If he made up his mind about something, you could not move him. Why, at six she had been able to repeat whole passages from Shakespeare by heart. Teddy could hardly remember two lines together.

She had set him to learn a few simple verses from her favorite, William Blake. He stood at her knee reciting it.

"*No, no, let us play, for yet it is day,*
And we cannot go to sleep;
Besides, in the sky the little birds fly,
And the hills are all covered with . . ."

He stopped.

"With what, Teddy?"

"Master Teddy don't know."

"Something white, Teddy."

"Snow?"

"No, no. Does snow rhyme with 'sleep'?"

"Paper?"

"No. Now I'm not going to the theatre until you say the right word. What are the hills covered with?"

"People."

"Teddy, you are a very naughty boy."

"Grass? Trees?"

"Are grass or trees white?"

And so it went, with Edy murmuring "Sheep, Teddy," under her breath, and Teddy obstinately refusing to say it, until they were both in tears at his defiance.

The boy needed a father. There were times during these months when she had a tremendous longing to be reconciled with her parents, with all her brothers and sisters, who were growing up without her. Wasn't it absurd that Edy and Teddy should have so many aunts and uncles about whom they knew absolutely nothing?

Help came from Tom Taylor. He had always been fond of Ellen and in his heart felt some responsibility for that unhappy child marriage. After all, he had brought them to the studio, thinking of Kate and never dreaming that it would be Ellen who would captivate the artist's eye. He went to see Watts and persuaded him of his injustice toward the girl wife he had treated so badly. In the autumn of 1877 Watts finally divorced her. At last she was free of the past.

The decree was made absolute when they were in the midst of rehearsals for *Olivia,* which had been adapted from Oliver Goldsmith's novel, *The Vicar of Wakefield,* by an extraordinary

Irishman. Poet, painter, and playwright, William Gorman Wills always looked as if he had slept in his clothes. More often than not, his face was smeared with charcoal or streaked with paint. His pockets bulged with tubes of oil paint, brushes, pencils, and dirty, stained envelopes on which he scribbled down his plays. Wills was a curious mixture, an aristocrat who could sit at rehearsals eating a raw onion with as much enthusiasm as any peasant and yet whose ideas were magnificent and filled with delicacy and feeling. His untidy studio was the haunt of down-and-outs, beggars, out-of-work models, all of whom ate his food, slept on his dilapidated sofa, always ready to pocket the money that with absent-minded generosity he handed out to anyone who seemed to need it. Ellen grew very fond of him.

It was after visiting him one day that she and Charles went on to Chelsea to see Whistler's portrait of Henry Irving in the role of Philip II of Spain. The studio was freezing. Whistler as always was deeply in debt. No one would buy his pictures and there was never any money to spare for fuel. Kelly impatiently urged her to come away, but she stood in front of the painting, shivering but fascinated. The superb study in black, gray, and silver had caught the essence of the performance, the quiet malignity and cruelty, the icy brilliance.

"You know," she said slowly, "when I saw him play this part in *Queen Mary* for the first time, in that scene where poor Mary Tudor pours out her heart to him, I began to believe in the power of an actor to create as well as to interpret. Tennyson's play did not suggest half of what Irving put into it."

"He doesn't like the picture," remarked Whistler carelessly. "He only agreed to let me paint it because I begged him to do so."

Ellen smiled. Maybe even the dedicated Mr. Irving liked to think of himself as the handsome young man of every woman's dream.

In the meantime, she was enjoying working on *Olivia.* It was a charming, sentimental story of an innocent girl wronged by the wicked squire, a part played to perfection by a young actor to whom she had taken an immediate liking.

William Terriss had been midshipman, tea planter, engineer, sheep farmer, and horse breeder. The daredevil spirit of the adventurer looked out of his insolent eyes. He had Byronic good looks. As Squire Thornhill he was precisely the charming, reckless, unworthy creature who always gets his own way, as apparently Terriss himself had done all through his life. He made her laugh at rehearsal, telling her that when he was only a child he said one morning to his mother, "Give me five pounds or I'll throw myself out of the window," and she actually believed him, calling out, "Come back, come back and I'll give you anything you want!"

To Ellen's amusement, this audacious young man who was fond of performing cowboy tricks on his horse when he went riding in Richmond Park was nevertheless paralyzed with nerves on opening night. Badly in need of reassurance herself, it was she who had to give him courage. Neither of them need have suffered any anxiety. *Olivia* was an instantaneous success and Ellen's photographs in her pretty eighteenth-century dresses were in every magazine and shop window. There was not a young woman in London who did not long to look just like her. "Olivia" bonnets and kerchiefs became the rage.

During the run of the play, and out of a great longing for safety and security, she made a rash and impulsive decision. She knew that she would never love anyone as she had loved Edward Godwin, but the children needed a father, they needed a name and status in strict Victorian society. Charles Kelly had been urging her to marry him, and out of all her suitors, he seemed the most sensible and practical.

One morning in spring they were married very quietly, no one guessing till they came back to the theatre that evening. A decent, respectable marriage was what her family had been waiting for. The erring daughter had come back to them and they flocked around her, though her father grumbled that she had thrown herself away. She was still his "Duchess" and could have married anyone, not an actor of whose abilities he had a very poor opinion.

Edy and Teddy found to their astonishment that they had a collection of bewildering new relatives. There was Grandmama, white-haired and dignified, with a most beautiful voice and lovely, gracious manner. She was a merry lady, Mamma had told them, so Teddy thought out his own little joke to amuse her when she came to tea for the first time. He had seen the clowns do it at the circus and everybody thought it splendid fun.

When she went to take her seat at the table, he quickly pulled the chair away and down toppled Grandmama, black silk skirts flying up around her. Only this time no one laughed. There was a dreadful silence. Then they all rushed to help her up.

Sarah had not lost her sense of humor. "That *was* fun!" she said, and smiled kindly at her new little grandson, scarlet-faced and very near to tears.

Then there was Grandpapa, gray-bearded but with a twinkling eye and ready for all kinds of games. There was Aunt Marion, who was an actress like Mamma, and Aunt Floss too, who was away on tour. Uncle Fred was only thirteen and still at school, but Uncle Charles worked in a big furniture firm, and Uncle Ben was in India. Uncle George had married a Catholic and had gone to live in France. Uncle Tom was the black sheep, always in trouble. No one mentioned him very much. Last but by no means least, there were Aunt Kate's daughters, four prim little girls from Campden Hill, heartily disliked by Edy and Teddy from their first meeting.

They did not really care very much for any of them, not while they had darling Mamma and Boo. Then there was Bo, who was really Miss Bocking, Boo's niece, who had come to live with them, and Miss Harries, who was housekeeper and governess. She was tiny, with thin gray hair and a lot of lace around a very scraggy neck, fastened with a gigantic brooch. She had a brusque manner and a passion for bringing home stray cats and dogs that made Mamma laugh but caused a lot of trouble in the kitchen. The children teased her, laughed at her, and loved her. Best of all, they liked their new father, especially Teddy. He was always ready for a manly game.

They had moved to a new and more comfortable home in Longridge Road, Earl's Court, closer to the theatres and not too far from Hyde Park, where Boo or Miss Harries would take the children for an afternoon walk. There was a flock of sheep to be looked at, ducks on the Serpentine to feed, and sometimes she took them to watch the riders prancing up and down Rotten Row on their splendid horses.

It was to this house, in July 1878, that a letter came one morning from Mr. Henry Irving.

Dear Miss Terry,

I look forward to the pleasure of calling on you on Tuesday next . . .

It took her by surprise. They had not met since that one time ten years before when neither had been impressed with the other.

A little nervously she took up her pen to write a reply.

My dear Mr. Irving,

I am at home all these hot days between eleven and three, and should be pleased indeed if you will call any day . . .

Why should he want to see her? It was rumored that since Bateman's sudden death his widow was giving up the Lyceum and Irving was going into management for himself. But though she had watched his career with interest and admiration, so far as she was aware, he had never seen her act. Could it be possible that he . . . No! She would not allow herself even to think of such a glorious possibility as acting with him. She tried to school herself to patience. Teddy and Edy were both walking on as village children in *Olivia*. There was always so much to be done, getting them ready and taking them with her to the theatre. Tuesday next must look after itself.

5

My Fairest Ophelia

OUTSIDE IN THE STREET it was grilling hot. London was experiencing one of its rare heatwaves and even with the curtains drawn the little front parlor at Longridge Road where Ellen waited for her visitor was stiflingly warm.

The very first thing she noticed about Henry Irving when Boo showed him into the room was how changed he was from the young man she had known ten years before. Gone was the stiff, ugly self-consciousness that had shut him in like the shell that closes around a lobster; gone, too, the inability to express himself and the savage pride born from years of hardship and ridicule. This was a man who had found himself at last. His manner was very quiet and gentle. Womanlike, she took in at one swift glance the thick curling hair black as a crow's wing, the fine forehead, the dark eyes like pools of melancholy in the pale face, the sensitive mouth.

They were both of them talking too quickly, exchanging trivialities about the weather, about his coming tour, about the little fox terrier he had brought with him, successor to Trin, who had been given him by the students of Trinity College after his season in Dublin and who had met a tragic end, choking on a chicken bone. With relief and a little amusement, Ellen realized that he was almost as nervous as she.

Then Charley, the dog, bored with the conversation and perhaps scenting one or other of Miss Harries's waifs and strays, decided to draw attention to himself. There was a momentary silence. Irving looked horrified at his pet's misbehavior. Ellen glanced at him and at Charley before she broke into irresistible laughter. Then they were both laughing, down on their knees with pan and brush from the hearth, the ice broken.

When he was gone, she could scarcely realize her good fortune. Was he really asking her to share in his tremendous venture as sole proprietor of the Lyceum? She did not quite believe it until the offer came in writing. He was inviting her to be his leading lady at a salary of forty guineas a week, with a benefit night to be shared with him which could bring in two hundred pounds or more. It was security for herself and for the children, and more than that, it was working in close partnership with an actor she deeply admired.

First, of course, she must go on tour with Charles during the summer months as she had promised, but in December she would join Irving to play Ophelia to his Hamlet.

Already from greenroom gossip Ellen knew a great deal about Henry Irving.

John Henry Brodribb was forty, nine years older than herself. He was born in the small village of Keinton Mandeville in Somerset on February 6, 1838. His father, a traveling salesman, was so poor that he was forced to move to Bristol in a desperate search for a new livelihood, and his mother, fearing the unhealthy life of the city for her only child, sent him to her sister in Cornwall. Aunt Sarah was married to Isaac Penberthy, a generous-hearted giant of a man, successful and well-to-do, the manager of four tin mines.

Halsetown was situated in a haunted and desolate countryside. At that time the extreme west of Cornwall was still remote and cut off from the rest of England. Outside the mining village lay dark hills and stretches of bleak moorland dotted with ancient monoliths and weird gray stone circles going back to pagan times where legend said the little people lived and fairies danced on Midsummer Eve. Only a few miles away the long green breakers of the Atlantic Ocean beat ceaselessly against the bare rocky shores.

The boy's imagination was stirred by the old customs still surviving among this Celtic people. Every Christmas the Mummers appeared in the ancient play of St. George and the Dragon. There were the Guise Dancers in their fantastic costumes. There were plays in the tiny Assembly Rooms in St. Ives, sometimes even Shakespeare, and exciting melodramas with ghosts and murders that held him enthralled and sent him trembling home, creeping through the dark country lanes. On a visit to his parents in Bristol he saw a lion tamer drive a team of twenty-four horses through the streets and afterwards, dazzled and entranced, watched the splendid figure clad in a leopard skin, cool and daring, enter a den of raging lions.

Like his mother, his aunt Sarah was deeply religious. At

her knee he learned his daily lesson from the Bible. Out in the fields with the other children, he fascinated them with dramatic recitations, boasting of the time when he would be a great actor. They listened fearfully, a little scandalized, actors were beings from another world, a dangerous and sinful one.

Once he and his two cousins played an antic trick on an old woman who called herself a witch. Dressed up in masks, horns, and forked tails, they appeared one night at her bedside, terrifying her with the same threats of demons and hellfire with which she had made the lives of the village children miserable.

When he was eleven, his uncle died suddenly and so Johnnie was sent to join his parents in the city of London, where his father had found work as caretaker of a big building in Broad Street. His passionate ambition to be an actor, growing stronger every day, was sternly frowned on by his mother. She was a strict Methodist and fiercely opposed to anything connected with the stage. In her opinion it was a path that led direct to damnation. But at school the headmaster encouraged the boy's budding talent, and just before his twelfth birthday, as a special treat and much against his mother's wish, his father took him to see the great Samuel Phelps play Hamlet at Sadler's Wells.

He was never to forget that magical night. The memory of it remained with him during the six weary years he worked from nine to seven every day as a very junior clerk in a firm of lawyers. While he refilled the inkpots, put out new blotting paper, sharpened the quill pens, and laboriously copied the long letters filled with dull legal language, he dreamed of the parts he would play, the great triumphs, the audience's rapturous applause.

Tall, thin, and lanky, he had few of the qualities an actor must possess. He moved awkwardly, his legs were too thin.

"Spindleshanks," his schoolmates called him, and some of them had laughed jeeringly at the stammer he had fought so hard to overcome. All he had was the genius that burned inside him, the flame of his ambition, and an unshakable belief in his own future. Every spare minute he had he worked at improving his speech. He joined a dramatic group, he took lessons in elocution. He went without food to pay for them and to buy books. Having left school at thirteen, he was forced to educate himself.

Greatly daring, and without telling his parents, he would visit the Adelphi Theatre, home of melodrama, with the uneasy feeling that he was being wicked and the gallery would probably fall into the pit for his special punishment, but all the same so fascinated that he could not stir from his seat and went back again and again.

Suddenly and unexpectedly he had his chance. His uncle Thomas, his father's brother, came into a little money and gave him a hundred pounds on his eighteenth birthday. An actor who had seen him play with his amateur dramatic group gave him a letter of introduction to a stock company. It was now or never. He did not hesitate. He gave up his job, though his employer, a kindly man, tried hard to make him realize his folly. Breaking the news to his parents was more difficult. His mother, whom he loved, never forgave him, convinced that his chosen profession would be his ruin. His father, bolder and more adventurous, was inclined to admire his son's courage and enterprise.

So many things had to be decided. A new name had to be found. Who ever heard of an actor called Brodribb? He resolved to use his own second name and after a great deal of thought chose Irving, partly after Edward Irving, a noted evangelist whose sermons he had been forced to swallow in his childhood, partly after the American writer, Washington Irving, whose *Sketch Book* had been one of his boyhood favorites.

A large portion of that precious hundred pounds had to be spent on what was then an essential part of an actor's wardrobe: a selection of wigs, buckles, feathers, lace, silk stockings, sham jewelry, and three different types of sword—all very necessary in the romantic costume plays which were the fashion in the provincial theatres.

That evening in Broad Street he hung the court sword with its jeweled hilt at the foot of his bed and from time to time during the night hours struck a match to marvel at his new treasure—a stage knight performing his vigil before his tinsel and pasteboard arms.

In the morning, with his meager possessions packed in a basket and a few pounds in his pocket, he took the train to Sunderland, far away in the north of England. He would have to live as best he could, for he was to be paid no salary until he had proved his worth.

In the year 1856, when Ellen was showing her childish promise as Mamillius in *The Winter's Tale,* Henry Irving played a tiny part in the same play at Sunderland, so paralyzed with stagefright on the first night that his half-conquered stammer caught up with him and he could scarce utter a word. He fled from the stage overcome with bitter shame and a raging anger at his own failure.

Some quality in him, his determination, his capacity for hard work, awoke the pity of two actors in the company. Sam Johnson and Tom Mead took him in hand. They poured out good advice, restoring his shattered self-confidence, giving him back the courage and strength to go on. Overcome with gratitude, he exclaimed, "If ever I rise, I shall not forget this."

Tom Mead, who had grown old in the harsh selfish world of

the theatre, smiled at this awkward, stammering newcomer with his ambitious dreams that would surely never be realized. He had heard speeches like that before. Now, twenty-two years later, the promise would be fulfilled. They were both to be with him at the Lyceum. Tom Mead, with his hawklike nose and deep-set eyes, was playing the Ghost of Hamlet's father.

By the time he was twenty-one, Irving had played 481 different parts. He had fought his way through years of harsh criticism, starvation, and hard-won triumph. Out of a tiny salary, he had never failed to send his father what he could. The old man lived to see his son's first great success in *The Bells* before he died in 1876.

Irving was fighting still, but as a general now, not in the ranks. At last he was to enter into his inheritance.

Before joining the company, Ellen had traveled down to Birmingham at his request to see again the production of *Hamlet* in which she was so soon to take part.

In her diary she wrote, "He played—I say it without vanity—for me. We players are not above that weakness . . . if ever anything inspires us to do our best it is the presence in the audience of some fellow-artist . . . the response flies across the footlights to us like a flame."

In four years, she thought, he had perfected his performance. Someone had commented unkindly, "Oh, Irving only makes Hamlet a love poem!" Was it true? She watched closely the scenes she would play with him. With what passionate longing his hands hovered over Ophelia in the nunnery scene. How brilliantly he spoke the advice to the players. He was swift and direct, but what infinite variety he had. He kept three things going at once, the antic madness, the sanity, and the sense of theatre. This Prince's feet might be on the ground, but his head reached to the stars.

The Lyceum, with Drury Lane and the Royal Opera House, Covent Garden, stood just north of the Strand, halfway between the City of London, where the rich Victorian merchants made their millions, and the West End with its fine houses, gardens, restaurants, and playhouses, where they lived and amused themselves.

The theatre was the third building to stand on this site since the first hall had been erected in 1765. During its time it had housed a succession of great actors and actresses, as well as opera, exhibitions of art, a balloon display, waxworks, and a conjuring show. Once it had been burned to the ground but had risen again from its ashes. Now under its new manager, it was to start a new life, one that would give its name an imperishable glory before the theatre faded into obscurity again.

Behind the Lyceum lay a network of dark narrow alleys, rotting tenements, squalid taverns, and decaying shops, their windows stuffed with soiled, worn-out goods, a district which Ellen tried to avoid or hurried through as quickly as she could.

The overcrowded slums, the clusters of half-starved children, the smell of poverty, reminded her of the dark grim towns of the industrial north. They were the other side of the picture, the depressing and terrible contrast to the rich Victorian prosperity, which as yet no government had seriously attempted to alleviate.

But she was not thinking of these things on the cold morning in December when she set out for her first rehearsal. Of Irving the actor she felt she already knew a great deal, but of Henry the man, reserved, withdrawn, shut up within himself, she knew scarcely anything. Common gossip said that his marriage was unhappy, that he was parted from his wife and two sons, that he had treated her abominably. She wondered how true it was. She was curious, a little apprehensive, still in considerable awe of him.

The decorators had not yet finished with the theatre. The seating was being made more comfortable. For the first time the hard wooden benches of the pit and gallery were being provided with backs. The dingy auditorium was being repainted in sage green and turquoise blue.

There was barely a fortnight to opening night. Though Irving had gathered around him a company of experienced players, he was an exacting and tireless producer. Rehearsals were long and arduous. They went on all day without a break, sometimes extending into the night. The actors snatched a bite of food when they could or went without. The Guv'nor, as they called him, usually went without.

She had met some old friends in the company. Mr. Chippendale, who had been more than fifty years on the stage and had once taught her to curtsy, was playing Polonius. He stood beside her in the stalls one day watching Irving on the stage. Though he had played Hamlet numberless times, he still rehearsed with cloak and sword. He demanded perfection from himself as well as from others.

"He has never spared himself," grunted old Mr. Chippendale half admiringly, and went on to tell her that in 1864, when Irving had first attempted the part, he had traveled from Manchester to Birmingham after his evening performance and arrived on Chippendale's doorstep, pale and exhausted, at two o'clock in the morning, begging him to tell him how Edmund Kean had played Hamlet. All night they had worked on it, and in the early hours of the morning he had hurried off to catch his train. He had to be back in Manchester for the afternoon rehearsal.

Such intense concentration was almost frightening. Ellen worked hard at her parts. She thought about them and studied them, but she had other interests, her home, her children, her friends. Irving was obsessed with the theatre. He thought of nothing else.

"We must start this play as a living thing," he said one morning, and she watched him working on the opening scenes until his face grew taut and livid with fatigue and yet in some strange way still remained beautiful. She could not endure to see him exhaust himself with such small result.

"Give it up," she said, greatly daring. "It's no better."

"Yes, it's a little better," he answered quietly, "and so it's worth doing."

The only one not included in this passionate concentration on detail was poor Ophelia, and she was desperately worried about her own performance. She had already visited an asylum to study those whose minds had gone astray, but found no help for Ophelia's mad scene until just as she was leaving she caught sight of a young girl staring vacantly at a blank wall. Suddenly without warning she threw up her hands and sped across the room like a swallow, the movement as poignant as it was beautiful. Thinking it over afterward, it seemed to her that an actor must imagine first and observe afterward.

"It is no good observing life and bringing the result to the stage without selection, without a definite idea," she wrote in her diary. "The imagination must come first, the realism afterwards."

Irving was always quiet with her, always gentle, he never stormed or raged or lost his temper, yet he was formidable and he always got his own way. She found this to her cost when she plucked up courage to speak to him about her costumes. Anxious not to be flustered at the last moment, she had gone ahead without consulting him. Now she told him they were already finished.

"Finished?" he said. "Very interesting. What colors are they?"

"In the first scene I wear a pinkish dress. It's all rose-colored with her. Her father and brother love her. The Prince loves her—so she wears pink."

"Pink," he repeated thoughtfully.

"In the nunnery scene I have a pale gold, amber dress—the most beautiful color," she went on enthusiastically. "The material is a church brocade. It will tone down the color of my hair. In the last scene I wear a transparent black dress."

"I see. In mourning for her father."

"No, not exactly that. I think red was the mourning color of the period. But black seems to me right—like the character, like the situation."

At that moment they were joined by old Walter Lacy, who had been with Charles Kean when she was still a child and who was now advising Irving on the production.

"Miss Terry has been telling me of her dresses," said Irving quietly. "She intends to wear black in the mad scene." Lacy looked startled, but his chief went on before he could speak. "Ophelias generally wear white, don't they?"

"I believe so," Ellen answered. "But black is more interesting."

"I should have thought you would look much better in white."

"Oh no," she answered decisively.

THE NEW YORK PUBLIC LIBRARY PICTURE COLLECTION

Henry Irving as Macbeth, drawn by V. W. Bromley for THE LONDON ILLUSTRATED NEWS, 1875

He said nothing more, but a little later Lacy sought her out.

"You didn't really mean that you are going to wear black in the mad scene?"

"Yes, I did. Why not?"

"Why not! My God, Miss Terry! There must be only one black figure in this play and that's Hamlet."

She was overcome at her stupidity. What a blundering donkey he must think her. There she was, thinking herself such an expert on colors and costumes after working with Edward Godwin, and Irving had hit at once on the right dramatic effect by instinct.

It was just like the music. He did not know one note from the other, but he knew precisely what was needed for the play.

"Change it! Patch it together, indeed!" roared Hamilton Clarke, the musical director, storming out of the theatre after his work had received severe criticism. "Mr. Irving knows nothing about music or he wouldn't ask me to do such a thing!"

The next day he was back, the score altered, saying humbly, "Upon my soul, it *is* better. The Guv'nor was perfectly right."

After these experiences it required real courage to tackle him again, but time and time again he would skip their scenes when they came to them, so that she was utterly miserable about her own performance.

"I am very nervous about my first appearance with you," she said one day. "Couldn't we rehearse our scenes?"

"We shall be all right," he said lightly.

His blind confidence in her terrified her, and her apprehension grew worse and worse as the opening night, December 30, approached.

All the seats had long been sold out. Everyone's nerves were tense. Ellen, wrought up with anxiety, did not know how much

Irving had risked on this venture. The costs had been very high. Bram Stoker, his business manager, a young Irishman who had given up his job in the Civil Service to join him at the Lyceum, stared at his account book in dismay. The overdraft at the bank stood at twelve thousand pounds, and Irving faced the future heavily in debt, his sole assets his belief in his own genius and Ellen's charm, beauty, and talent—and she was convinced that she had failed him.

She fled from the theatre as soon as her own part was done. She was not beside him for the final curtain, when the applause rocked the Lyceum and the laurel wreaths and bouquets showered down upon the stage. Instead, she was driving up and down the Embankment in a hansom cab, with Boo beside her.

"I have failed! I have failed!" she said over and over again, the tears pouring down her face, very nearly ready to throw herself into the dark river.

Gently, Boo persuaded her to come home, where she sat before the dying fire, beset with a feeling of hopelessness.

At midnight there came a ring at the bell. Unbelievably, it was Irving himself, worried at her absence, holding out his hands to her. "My fairest, sweetest, loveliest Ophelia."

The critics the next day spoke of "her singular power of depicting intensity of feeling." They praised the beauty and innocence of the early scenes, contrasting them with the stark tragedy of her madness, but Irving's praise meant more than any of them.

"How Shakespeare must have dreamed when he was able to write a part like Ophelia knowing it had to be played by a boy," he said to Bram Stoker after the third performance. "Conceive his delight and gratitude if he could but have seen Ellen Terry in it!"

When she looked back on her first season at the Lyceum, it seemed to Ellen that this was a period of nothing but intense and concentrated work, but how splendid it was, how well worth doing. She was completely absorbed by her work, even though she grew thin as a shadow. It was not easy, learning lines, studying, rehearsing, playing every night. It was hard to fit it all into life at Longridge Road and still find a little free time to devote to Edy and Teddy.

Then there was Charles. There was no place for him in Irving's theatre. He had always regarded himself as her leading man; he had a fine conceit of his ability as an actor and he greatly resented her interest growing away from him. She had promised to go on tour with him again in the summer, but in the meantime he had to find other work or mope at home. A feeling of tension grew between them.

Hamlet ran until April, to be followed by *The Lady of Lyons,* an old romantic drama by Lord Lytton, the famous historical novelist. It was the story of a proud aristocratic beauty and her humble lover, set in revolutionary France. She had played Pauline for a single performance in 1875 just after her striking success as Portia and she had won the highest critical praise for her performance. Now Irving revived it for her and himself played her lover.

It was not a great play and she was never satisfied with herself in it, but it was dramatic and exciting and the public flocked in to see the magnificent scenery and the splendid stage effects, particularly the hero's departure for the wars. Irving had recruited his army from the Brigade of Guards at a shilling an hour. The old theatrical trick never failed. The soldiers marched past the windows with banners flying and drums beating, then doubled back around the stage cloth, to march past again endlessly while the curtain rose and fell to rapturous applause.

And there were other, more serious productions. She saw for the first time Irving's performance in *The Bells,* in which she had no part. The spiritual and physical intensity of his acting held her enthralled. Mathias, the innkeeper, has murdered a rich Jew in order to save his family from grinding poverty. Haunted by his crime, he dreams in a macabre last act that he is being tried and condemned and reenacts the terrible scene of the murder when he hacked down the Jew as he came through the snow-covered fields in his sleigh. The scene fades into the morning of his daughter's wedding. It is time for him to take her to the church, but Mathias, still driven by the horror of his dream, does not hear them calling him. They break down the door. He staggers forward, clutching at the imaginary noose around his throat. His strangled cry, "Cut the rope! Take the rope from my neck!" chilled the blood as he fell forward dead, the sleigh bells still ringing in his tortured ears. For twenty minutes, alone on the stage, Irving held his audience spellbound.

He had a passion for these tragic and melancholy parts, she thought, and how splendid he was in them. There was a trace of extravagance in his acting, something his critics seized on to jeer at and make fun of, forgetting that it is a part of all great art. Only the mediocre, the ordinary, are afraid to go beyond the limit.

There was *Eugene Aram,* based on Thomas Hood's famous poem, in which she had a small but good part. It was another study of a conscience-stricken murderer, a schoolmaster this time, harassed to his death by blackmail. The last act was grimly and poetically staged, with a great cedar tree stretching its black arm across the stage like a finger of fate over the wretched man crouched on the grave of his victim. The Fate Tree, Irving called it. It had played a part in *Hamlet* and was destined to appear in a number of productions.

Louis XI was a play in which Charles Kean had achieved one of his greatest successes. Despite Ellen's allegiance to the actor she had admired as a child, she was quite won over by Henry's brilliant study of the ugly, spindle-shanked, ruthless, cunning "Spider" King who had ruled in France in the fifteenth century. Irving had no illusions about the quality of the play. "It's penny-plain, you know, tuppence-colored," he said about it one day. But his elaborate, picturesque, grotesque old tyrant king never failed to grip the audience for the next thirty years.

Ellen had settled into the theatre by now. She had got over her first fears, and her natural gaiety reasserted itself. Her radiant beauty, her irresistible charm made an indelible impression on the entire company and not least on Irving himself.

Intensely serious and dedicated to his art, he felt sometimes that he had invited a sylph or sprite to share his work with him. Except for her passionate interest in the theatre, she was in every way so different for him: she had so many outside interests, she lacked his concentration, she was easily distracted, apt to forward other people's interests rather than her own. Her swift transition from gay to grave sometimes bewildered him. At one moment she would be laughing and chattering in the green-room and a second later she would be playing a heart-rending scene, bathed in her own tears. Once he caught her sliding down the banisters from her dressing room. He smiled but did not seem able to get over it. She felt as if she had laughed in church. But all the same his admiration for her was unbounded.

She was so unlike other actresses. She never looked on herself as clever or even as a beauty, so she was never vain. She liked to dress well, but preferred her dresses to be easy and comfortable rather than in the height of fashion. She never fussed about her appearance, yet had the supreme quality of looking always lovely.

"You are so free from self-consciousness, so easy, what is your secret?" he asked her one day, and she told him frankly that she would have been paralyzed with stagefright if she had tormented herself the way he did, waiting for ten minutes in the wings, tense and nervous, for his entrance.

"Stay in your dressing room till the call boy comes for you," she advised him gravely.

He did not heed her immediately, but it marked a step forward in their friendship that he could bring himself to ask such a question.

If she forgot her lines or came late to rehearsal, as she did sometimes, not out of carelessness but because her life was so full of other important matters, he never reproached her. She would slide onto the stage hoping he had not noticed, but he never missed anything.

"You turn all your critics into lovers," he said to her once with his rare, attractive smile.

There were other revivals in which she had to play her part in this first season. She was Lady Anne to his Richard III. For two hundred years the play had been presented in a mutilated form, with the king played as a villainous hunchback. Daringly he had restored the full text, winning the approval of the Shakespearean scholars and playing Richard as a subtle study of ruthless enterprise with a devastating sardonic charm.

Then there was *Charles I*.

Long afterward Teddy remembered how at this time, when he was almost eight, his mother was always humming a particular tune and sometimes would sing a little song to him when she came to kiss him goodnight before she left for the theatre.

Golden slumbers kiss thine eyes,
Smiles awake you when you rise,
Sleep, pretty wanton, do not cry,
And I will sing a lullaby,
Lullaby, lullaby,
Lul—lulla—by

It was many years before he realized that it was Orlando Gibbons's lovely melody for Thomas Dekker's poem written in the early seventeenth century, and it was played by the orchestra as the royal barge glided across the stage at the end of Act One in *Charles I*.

The play had been written by Ellen's old friend, the wild Irishman, William G. Wills, and it centered around the last few years of the king's life, leading up to his execution. Henrietta Maria became one of Ellen's favorite parts.

"I've just returned from our last rehearsal of *Charles I*," she wrote to the author. "Coming home in the carriage, I have been reading the last act and I can't help writing to thank you and bless you for having written these five last pages. Never, never has anything more beautiful been written in English . . . they are perfection . . ."

Another Irishman, aged twenty-five and just come down from Oxford in a blaze of glory, thought so too. Night after night, a tall, heavily built young man called Oscar Wilde, with large, luminous eyes and a massive forehead, dressed in a black velvet coat, knee breeches, silk stockings, and frilled shirt with a pale green flowing tie, sat and worshipped in the pit or gallery, which was all he could afford.

The sonnet he sent her stood out from the hosts of admiring letters she received daily.

In the lone tent, waiting for victory,
She stands with eyes marred by the mists of pain
Like some wan lily over drenched with rain . . .

"Wan lily" . . . he had hit exactly on what she had been trying to convey. She sent him a warm letter of thanks.

Not all the critics were so lyrical in their praise. Henry James, the American novelist, was of the opinion that no English actors, and certainly neither Irving nor Ellen Terry, could touch the perfection of the Comédie Française. He wrote disparagingly, "She has charm, a great deal of a certain amateurish angular grace, a total want of what the French call *chic* and a countenance very happily adapted to the expression of pathetic emotion."

Ellen did not mind very much. The first season had been extremely successful, and she was lost in admiration of Irving as Charles I. Again and again she thought she had seen the best he could do, and still he surprised her. In her copy of the play she scribbled her impressions one night: "His stateliness—his gentleness—every inch a King. His beautiful hands—his face—his bearing—unlike most stage kings he never seems to be assuming dignity, he is very very simple."

She noticed too the brilliance of his makeup. He came on looking exactly like the Van Dyck portrait, but not with the help of nose paste, paint, and powder, but by a subtle accentuation of the lines of his face that assisted the expression from within.

I fear me I may sometimes fade from thee,
That when thy heart expelleth grey-stoled grief
I live no longer in thy memory;
Oh, keep my place in it for ever green
All hung with the immortelles of thy love . . .

Only Irving could speak such lines of farewell to his Queen so that the audiences were drowned in tears.

6

Lyceum Years

ROSE COTTAGE WAS one of a short row of little white houses a few miles out of London close beside the river Thames. The back windows looked out on the green stretches of Bushey Park. Sitting astride the windowsill, Edy and Teddy used to watch the deer treading their way daintily through the great trees. Sometimes to their excitement the stags would fight, grunting and roaring, heads lowered and antlers entangled. Afterward the children would run out, hunting eagerly for broken pieces of horn on the grass.

Now that she had money to spare, Ellen had taken the cottage as a country retreat from the heat and dust of Longridge Road. During the winter, mindful of the gaps left in her own education, she had sent Edy and Teddy to school in Earl's Court.

Mrs. Cole, the headmistress, was very advanced. She believed girls should be given the same education as boys and was a pioneer of co-education. Their schoolmates were the children of writers and artists. But at the cottage during the summer months they ran wild. In their blue and white checked pinafores, they would race up the road to the rose-red Tudor Palace of Hampton Court, built by Wolsey in the early sixteenth century and snatched by Henry VIII on the Cardinal's fall from power.

At the Lion Gate there was the confectioner where they bought delicious ices, and very soon they were firm friends with the old soldier who stood guard at the entrance. When there was a great crowd of tourists come to look over the palace and the gardens, they would help him to sell his picture postcards and bottles of ginger beer.

The magnificent grounds stretching down to the river became their playground. They would tell visitors about Mamma, who was acting in London, and show them the young trees which they had helped the gardeners to plant and had christened after the parts she played and the plays she was in: Ophelia, Portia, Charles I, Henrietta Maria. But what they enjoyed most was the famous Maze.

People had amused themselves in it for centuries, jostling and screaming at one another as they tried to find their way through the narrow green alleys to the center, shrieking with laughter like peahens. Then there would come a silence. Suddenly they were terrified. Perhaps they would never get out. It was then that the guide on his tall wooden crow's nest would call out, reassuring them, directing them to the right paths. Sometimes when he wanted a few minutes off he let the children take over from him. How they loved it.

"Turn to the right, the lady with the white hat," they would shout. "No, not that way! You've gone too far. You there, with the top hat, you're wrong, sir! Go back. That's right!"

It was rather like playing God. It was glorious fun.

What Teddy liked best was wandering through the state rooms of the palace with all the paintings of court ladies and handsome gentlemen with swords and wigs, and the lofty four-poster beds surmounted with gilded coronets and clusters of ostrich feathers.

What happened, he wondered as he stared up at them, when the doors were closed? What mystery lurked behind the embroidered bed curtains when darkness fell and shadows crept across the floor? Sometimes he would have a nightmare about it and wake up screaming. He was an imaginative child.

In September of 1879 a new visitor called one weekend at Rose Cottage, a tall man in a jaunty close-fitting jacket, a wide-brimmed hat tilted over one eye, and a lively terrier trotting at his heels. This was Mr. Irving, Mamma told them, from the Lyceum Theatre. Gravely he shook hands with them. Edy's sharp eyes noticed that her stepfather, Charles Kelly, left the room as soon as the guest was shown in, but Teddy was deeply impressed with the quiet smile, the twinkle in the dark eyes, and the calm, friendly way in which he spoke to him man to man.

He had come to talk to Mamma about his new production of *The Merchant of Venice,* but over tea, listening to the children chatter about their adventures in the gardens, he told them the sad story of a little boy he had known.

"He was a lonely lad," he said, "not like you two lucky ones, and sent out by his aunt one day to call home the cows, he saw a sweetly pretty lamb looking down at him from the field above the tall hedge. He had always loved the lamb in his Bible lessons, so his heart went out to it. He scrambled up the steep muddy bank, threw his arms round the little creature's neck, and kissed it. Do you know what happened? The lamb bit him."

Teddy rolled about, exploding with laughter. Irving smiled down at Ellen's plump, rosy-cheeked son.

"This same boy," he went on gravely, "had very thin legs, so skinny in fact that all the other children roared with laughter at him so that, even when he grew up, he so hated to be found ridiculous that if ever he had to show them, he wore a padding under his stockings."

Teddy was still giggling, but Edy, who was older, saw the little smile that flitted across her mother's face and guessed shrewdly that Mr. Irving was talking about himself.

Presently, when the children had romped out into the garden, taking Charley the dog with them, Ellen met his eyes across the tea table. "Oh, Henry," she exclaimed, "how can you be so foolish! What do you want with fat podgy legs when you have so much?"

How strange, she thought. A year ago she would never have dared to say such a thing to him. Now very gradually with her he was losing the sensitive reserve with which he had guarded himself from hurt. He has no idea how handsome he really is; he uses his fine hands quite unconsciously and he carries himself like a prince, she was thinking to herself as she listened to him telling her of his trip to Venice that summer and the old trader he had seen in Tunis in the marketplace. At one moment he had been tearing his clothes in rage, writhing and fawning in the dust of the road, and a few seconds later he had stalked away with a kingly pride, behind his mule team. It had given him a completely new idea of how to play Shylock.

Ellen would be glad to be back at the Lyceum. She had spent

three months on tour with Charles, but it had not been a happy time. He was deeply jealous and resentful of her new interest. There had been quarrels. It worried her that now and again he was drinking too much.

Yet he could still be loving and thoughtful. He played her husband in a play called *Butterfly* and in the last act had to show her a locket with the picture of her son. One night he substituted for the stage property a beautiful silver locket with two tiny colored photographs of Edy and Teddy. She had burst into tears when she opened it. She knew that he realized why she had married him, and was unhappy because of it. She felt guilty because she had so little in common with him. She had never loved him and now they were pursuing such different paths. There was no real place for him in her new life.

At the beginning of October, Irving read *The Merchant of Venice* to the assembled company in the greenroom. This was his usual custom. He worked on the play himself until he had made up his mind about every detail, and then how splendidly he read it, Ellen thought. No need for him to give out the names of the characters, there was never the least doubt who was speaking. Swiftly and surely he acted out all the parts and his actors did well to take note how he played his own part, for never again until the first night, though he rehearsed with them, would he show his conception so clearly and completely.

After the reading he gave out the scripts, handwritten or, more often than not, in the case of Shakespeare, privately printed and bound.

On this particular Thursday, the actors dismissed, he led

Ellen away into the jumble of passages behind the stage to show her what had been done during her absence.

Certain old lumber rooms had been cleaned out and redecorated. At the beginning of the century, he told her, the Sublime Society of Beefsteaks used to hold their meetings in the Lyceum. It was an eating and conversation club going back to the days of Queen Anne and it had once numbered Sheridan among its members, as well as other men distinguished in the arts and sciences. Its president, the Duke of Norfolk, used to preside at the suppers wearing a hat crowned with feathers which had once adorned the head of David Garrick.

Irving had every intention of reviving the Beefsteak suppers, only with something more varied and interesting than the plain steaks and green salad washed down with port wine which had served the original members.

This was a side of Irving she had not yet seen, the man who enjoyed entertaining, who was a princely host and who had a sardonic and witty turn of humor at his command for such occasions. She had a feeling she was never to find out everything about this surprising and fascinating man.

Rehearsals followed a regular daily pattern. Irving, with Bram Stoker and his stage manager, H. J. Loveday, ruled the company with firm discipline. He expected hard work, integrity, and ungrudging loyalty, and in return his actors always found the Guv'nor just. Everything was done for their comfort in dressing rooms and greenroom and no one in trouble ever appealed to his kindness or generosity in vain.

It amused Ellen to see how eagerly they watched his arrival from his rooms in Grafton Street every morning. If he wore a silk hat, indicating he had some social engagement, they knew they were in for a comparatively calm day. If he wore his wide-brimmed, soft felt hat—his "storm" hat, they called it—then look out for squalls and tempests if things did not go right.

There were barely three weeks to go before they opened. Hawes Craven, the scenic artist, had replaced his brown, paint-splashed bowler hat with a bright-red bandana handkerchief, always a sign of intense and concentrated work.

Ellen plunged joyously into studying Portia once again. From her childhood Shakespeare had been her dearest love. Women owed him a vast debt of gratitude, she used to say, for the marvelous way he had drawn them. Rosalind, Beatrice, Viola—they were all girls of strong character, high-spirited, quick-witted, and resourceful. That was how she saw Portia, a great lady of the Italian Renaissance, independent of spirit, gay, mocking, charming, and at the same time very much in love.

She soon became aware that she must revise her earlier idea of the part if she was to fit in with Irving's Shylock. He was playing the Jew not as the traditional grotesque villain, the grasping, miserly moneylender, raging and ranting, but as a man of high dignity, intensely proud of his race and fiercely resentful of the arrogant young Venetians with their careless condescension which did not hide their contempt. It was an intellectual study, subtle, unusual, and at times deeply tragic.

To act with those whose genius is equal or greater than one's own is a stimulus to all good actors. She rose to meet the challenge magnificently. The trial scene became a superb battle between them in which neither had the victory.

Working so closely together, they grew more intimate. Irving had discovered that her experience with Watts and Godwin had taught her a great deal about color and design. She had a far wider knowledge of the world of art outside the theatre than he had. He began to consult her in matters of costume and setting as well as in other, more personal problems.

Was it true, he asked her one day, what the critics said about his mannerisms, the way he spoke, the way he walked?

She admired him far too much to answer with easy flattery. She told him plainly and frankly what she thought, and because, so far as theatre was concerned, their interests were identical, he found that he could trust her criticisms, take them to heart and profit by them. His almost childlike eagerness for any suggestion that might improve his interpretation astonished her. He was never obstinate about taking advice and he never ceased working on a part, never ceased adding to the tiny details that built it into an outstanding creation.

She had discovered something else about him too. On the first night, feeling a little more relaxed than usual, she noticed the good-looking, handsomely dressed woman who sat in the stage box.

"That is Mrs. Irving," they whispered to her. She stared at her curiously. He had never said a word about his personal tragedy, but others in the company had told her a good deal. He had married Florence O'Callaghan in 1869 when he was only a struggling actor and she the daughter of a surgeon general in the Indian Army. It had been an unhappy marriage and had lasted a bare two years despite the birth of a son. From the first there had been a lack of understanding between them. His wife had fallen in love with a striking and unusual actor and then had bitterly resented the absorption in his work that kept him so often away from her. There were quarrels and reconciliations. He was too single-minded, too devoted to the theatre, to be an easy man to live with, but he had genuinely tried to give her all he could, and he adored his baby son.

Just before the birth of their second child, there came his first triumphant achievement in *The Bells,* the kind of magical night which comes to an actor perhaps only once in a lifetime, the moment when he realizes that, after years of struggle, success is within his grasp, the world is at his feet.

As they drove home after the first-night party, he turned to her, exhausted but happy and exalted, longing to plan the future with her, perhaps remembering how his idol, Edmund Kean, had felt in his hour of glory.

He put his arm around her. "Well, Flo my dear, we too shall soon have our carriage and pair."

Incapable of sharing his dreams, jealous of the praise that had been lavished on him, she answered sharply, cruelly. "Are you going on making a fool of yourself like this all your life?"

It hit him like a physical blow. He stopped the brougham, got out without a word, and ordered the driver to go on without him. He never returned home or spoke to her again. In that hour the last link in his armor of reserve was forged. He would not allow himself to be hurt again.

There was a deed of separation. He never spoke of the weeks of misery he endured or of the pain he felt at being parted from his two sons, who were to be brought up to despise their father. Harry and Laurence were very nearly the same age as Edy and Teddy. Ellen's warm, generous spirit overflowed with sympathy. She had suffered herself, but at least she had the joy of the children.

All this flitted through her mind as she watched the silent figure sitting with her hands clasped in her lap while the applause thundered around them. Not a gesture of kindness or praise for the man who had just given one of the finest performances of his life.

Magnificently presented and dressed, the production called

forth a storm of acclamation and criticism. Ellen in her golden dress that she wore as lightly as if it were gossamer was praised for the nobility and purity of her playing, for her essential womanliness. The Lord Chief Justice himself commended her brilliant legal style in the trial scene.

There were disapproving voices too. Henry James sternly criticized Irving for playing the Jew for pathos, and went on to say of Ellen: "Her manner of dealing with the delightful speeches of Portia with all their play of irony, wit and temper, savours, to put it harshly, of the schoolgirlish. Miss Terry's Mistress of Belmont giggles too much, plays too much with her fingers, is too free in her relations with Bassanio . . ."

She was being called to account everywhere for the freedom of her acting. Another critic remarked sourly: "There was altogether too much of what Rosalind calls 'a coming-on disposition' in Miss Terry's bearing towards her lover."

Neither Irving nor she resented criticism if it was constructive. They were prepared to learn from it, but both their performances had emerged out of deep study of the play. Shakespeare's Shylock surely could have more than one interpretation, and she disliked any suggestion of indelicacy in her acting, especially when she had the poet's own authority for her manner of playing. Did he not make Portia say before Bassanio has chosen the right casket:

One half of me is yours, the other half yours—
Mine own, I would say; but if mine, then yours,
And so all yours.

Dr. Furnivall, the great scholar, confirmed her interpretation. "Your whole conception and acting of the character are so true to Shakespeare's lines," he wrote, "that one longs he could be here to see you. A lady gracious and graceful, handsome, witty, loving and wise, you are his Portia to the life."

Controversy only added to the play's popularity. It ran for seven months, a record in those days, and on the hundredth night Irving gave a great supper party to some three hundred friends and acquaintances. She stood beside him to receive them in the new Beefsteak Room. Behind them hung a splendid portrait head of Edmund Kean, and Whistler's painting of Philip II, which Irving had bought for three hundred pounds when the unfortunate artist went bankrupt. In the meantime, the stage was being transformed into a great scarlet and white pavilion lit by two glittering chandeliers.

As each guest sat down to supper, with the champagne bubbling in the glasses, he was presented with a copy of the play, bound in white vellum and decorated with gold. Among the guests was a dazzled and fascinated Oscar Wilde, whose new poem had just arrived on her dressing table.

For in that gorgeous dress of beaten gold
Which is more golden than the golden sun,
No woman Veronese looked upon
Was half so fair as thou whom I behold.
Yet fairer when with wisdom as your shield
The sober-suited lawyer's gown you donned,
And would not let the laws of Venice yield
Antonio's heart to that accursed Jew—
O Portia, take my heart; it is thy due:
I will not quarrel with the Bond.

Lord Houghton, the guest of honor, a peer of literary tastes and a minor poet, in proposing Irving's health tactlessly deplored managements who encouraged long runs of plays and chided his host for "whitewashing" the villainous Shylock. A shudder ran around the company. How would the Guv'nor respond to such an unexpected snub? But they need not have feared.

"Henry's answer was delightful," wrote Ellen in her diary. "He spoke with good sense, good humour and good breeding, and it was all spontaneous."

The shy, awkward, stammering boy from the provinces had come a long way toward establishing the position of an actor in good society far from the "rogues and vagabonds" of earlier ages.

Ellen played one more new part that season—Iolanthe, blind daughter of a Danish king, whose sight is miraculously restored to her. It was an old romantic one-act play which Irving commissioned William G. Wills to rewrite for him. He put it on solely for Ellen, knowing very well that the part of her lover, Count Tristan, was not one in which he was at his best. He presented it with all his usual care and had his reward. She was highly praised for the exquisite tenderness of her performance. Played on the same night as *The Merchant of Venice*, it made a vivid contrast to her Portia and became one of the most popular plays in the Lyceum repertory.

In July the season came to an end. Ellen left to go on her summer tour with Charles, and Irving went for a short holiday to Southsea and was nearly blown to pieces.

Ellen did not know whether to laugh or cry when she read his letter. He and Bram Stoker had taken a boat out for a short sail and about half a mile from the shore there was a sudden fearful explosion. When at last the boat righted itself, they found themselves drenched and shoals of dead fish were floating on the surface of the water. They had sailed into a minefield, part of the naval maneuvers from nearby Portsmouth.

The boatman implored them to return to the shore, but Irving calmly lighting a cigar, said coolly, "Why? The mines here have been fired and we don't know where the others are. Let's stay where we're safe and enjoy ourselves." And so they did, for the rest of the afternoon, while mines exploded and cannons roared all round them.

Ellen wondered how the navy would have felt if their latest inventions for ruling the waves had blown up London's favorite tragedian.

In a room in Eaton Place, in early December, Tennyson was reading aloud his two-act tragedy, *The Cup*. He had taken the theme from Plutarch—the story of Camma, wife of a Galatian prince who is murdered by Synorix, a fellow countryman who has sold himself to the Roman conqueror and desires Camma for himself. The last act takes place in the temple of the Goddess Artemis, where Camma has taken refuge. There she avenges her husband by promising to marry his slayer and, when he comes to the temple for the wedding ceremony, insisting on his making a libation to the gods. She offers him the poisoned cup she has prepared, drinking from it first herself, and so destroys them both.

The poet was over seventy, an untidy, shaggy man in his great Spanish cloak. "A dilapidated Jove," someone had called him with his high domed forehead and flowing beard. His voice was a low, rumbling monotone, except when a woman was speaking, when it rose up to a shrill, high-pitched note he could not sustain.

Ellen, deeply impressed with the beauty of the verse, was suddenly horrified to see Edy, perched on Irving's knee, making hideous grimaces over his shoulder at Hallam, the poet's son. She shook her head disapprovingly at her daughter, but Irving was grinning, and to make matters worse, Charley, at his feet, yawned hugely, struggled up, gave a very noisy shake, and then lay down again.

It was astonishing, thought Ellen, how the children had taken to Henry, especially Teddy. He was the last person she would have expected to be good with children, yet he had exactly the right manner, a mixture of indulgence and firmness. She had a sudden feeling of intense relief that he was there, steady as a rock, someone on whose advice and strength she knew she could rely.

For a moment her mind strayed from the reading to think back over the last few months with Charles. The tour should have been a happy one. They had good audiences and at Leeds she had for the first time played Beatrice in *Much Ado about Nothing,* a part she had long dreamed of making her own. But Charles had become impossible. It was like living with a steamroller, she thought indignantly to herself.

He wanted to dominate every part of her life, and she was too independent, her spirit needed freedom. She rebelled against the constraint. They clashed again and again, over her work at the Lyceum, over her growing friendship with Irving, even over the education of the children. Teddy, he said, was growing up too soft. He accused her of spoiling him. He strode about the house flourishing a horsewhip to show his authority, terrifying the child. Try as she would, she had not been able to keep him from drinking too much.

Uneasily, she felt she was not really fair to him, but when after they had been home only a few weeks he packed his bags one morning and stormed out of the house, she was happy to see him go. She would gladly give him half of what she earned if he would only stay away.

The reading was over. Edy was making impertinent remarks in far too loud a voice. Ashamed of her daughter's bad manners, Ellen tried to silence her, but Henry was looking mischievous. "Leave the child alone," he whispered. "She's quite right."

He had already made up his mind to put on *The Cup* in the New Year. It would provide Ellen and himself with two excellent parts, and there would be added prestige in producing a play by the Poet Laureate. While they were discussing certain aspects of the production, Ellen put forward the suggestion that had flitted through her mind during the reading. Why not ask Edward Godwin to design the costumes and settings? He had a wide knowledge of the period. He was exactly the person to create the right atmosphere, pagan, mysterious, and beautiful.

"If you think the idea is a good one," she said, "I will write to him on your behalf."

For a moment Irving could not answer. She had taken him aback. She was right, of course. It was an excellent suggestion, but how could anyone be so completely without resentment, so ungrudging toward the man who had caused her so much bitterness and pain? It was something he himself could never have done. He always found it difficult to forgive any injuries done to his friends.

He nodded at last, and his admiration, his growing appreciation of her, took a great leap forward. What a rare and lovely person she was, and how fortunate he was to have her beside him. There had been many attempts by other managements to lure her away, but she had refused them all.

William Terriss was also at the reading. Ellen had urged Irving to engage him, and here he was installed at the Lyceum and playing in *The Corsican Brothers* while they rehearsed *The Cup*. "Breezy Bill," they called him, and he was the same handsome, scatterbrained, charming daredevil he had been in *Olivia*, who feared nothing and no one.

It had looked at first as if his stay would be a short one. Rehearsing a duel with Irving one day, he had noticed that the limelight man was loyally keeping his chief in the beam and leaving the rest of the stage in darkness. Terriss lowered his sword. "Don't you think, Guv'nor, a few rays of the moon might fall on me? It shines equally, ye know, on the just and the unjust."

The rest of the company held their breath, waiting for the thunderbolt to fall. There was a momentary silence. Then Irving laughed. He had no liking for yes-men and the young man's independent spirit pleased him. He changed the lighting and ever after treated Terriss with an amused tolerance.

Writing of his childhood in later years, Teddy remembered the first time his mother took him to the Lyceum, and to his delight he was allowed to watch *The Corsican Brothers* from backstage. He gazed up at the tall canvas flats disappearing into the flies amid the countless ropes and pulleys that insured that one scene would melt into the next. He watched the trick of the ghost rising up from the cellar below through the trap to appear in a burst of spectral light. He was nearly nine. It was the beginning of his lifelong fascination with the theatre and he had no notion that the slim, brown-bearded man who was watching the scene painters at work on his designs for *The Cup* was the father he could not remember. He had been brought up in a circle of adoring women, and it was Irving who attracted him now and would soon become the ideal on which he would try to model himself.

In those days of hand-operated scenery, an army of stagehands performed miracles changing in record time a scene of open country into the marble-pillared Temple of Artemis with a ceiling of inlaid gold.

Ellen's robe as the priestess was a marvel of ingenuity. No material could be found to match Godwin's exquisite design except a hand-woven Indian silk sewn with small jewels which Ellen had seen at Liberty's, one of the great London stores. But it cost twelve guineas a yard and they needed twenty yards! Such lavish expenditure would have been considered wanton waste at the Lyceum.

"Give me the sample," said Arnott, the stage carpenter. In a few days he was back with an inexpensive material dyed to the exact shade of saffron. He had had wooden blocks made to print the pattern and decorated it with a few cheap spangles so that it looked better on the stage than the expensive original would have.

Ellen was never quite sure that she reached the full heights of tragedy in the last act. Like all true artists, she was rarely satisfied with herself. She fell short of her own imagining of the part, but the public did not think she had. They lavished praise on her and the production and Irving. Physically, he could not look the full-blooded, bull-necked tyrant of the classical statues which Tennyson had envisaged, but he created his own image.

"With a pale pale face, bright red hair, gold armour and a tiger skin, a diabolical expression and very thin crimson lips," wrote Ellen, "Henry looked handsome and sickening at the same time."

On the hundredth night, she sent Tennyson a replica of the Cup, made in silver from Godwin's design. It was three-handled, shaped like a pipkin, and stood on three legs.

The Cup was too short a play to fill an entire evening. With it they put on *The Corsican Brothers*, but it made a somber night's entertainment, so after a few weeks Irving substituted *The Belle's Stratagem*, a rollicking play from the eighteenth century. It was the first opportunity Ellen had at the Lyceum to show her skill in comedy, and she reveled in it. Laetitia Hardy plans to captivate her reluctant lover by first shocking him with the outrageous behavior of a saucy hoyden and then entrancing him by a sudden switch to charm and vivacity. Ellen was applauded for her versatility in turning so brilliantly from Camma to Laetitia on the same night, though she was never quite sure she liked the abrupt change from tragedy to comedy. What she did notice was how extremely funny Irving was as Doricourt, and the marvelous play of expression on his face.

In one scene she had to sing a delightful, teasing song to him, and when she went out to parties, she was often asked to repeat it. "No," she used to say, "it isn't a song. It's a look here, a gesture there, a laugh anywhere and Henry's face everywhere!"

Another elderly actor had come to join the company. She had known "Daddy" Howe, as she called him, since her earliest days. He had been on the stage so long that he remembered back to the time when it was lit by oil lamps, when if one smoked or flickered out, the servant of the theater had to come and relight it, right in the middle of the performance if need be. Irving called him the "agricultural" actor, because he was passionately attached to his little farm and turned up at rehearsals with stout gaitered legs and mud on his boots.

They had distinguished visitors too. There was Mr. Gladstone, Chancellor of the Exchequer. He liked to watch the plays from the wings, so a seat was prepared for him covered with red baize and protected against draft by a curtain. It was a place he was to occupy for many a performance.

Disraeli came, now Lord Beaconsfield, very old and frail but with an eye still for a pretty girl. He hinted that he would like to take one of the ladies of the chorus to supper and Bram Stoker had some difficulty explaining that the serious young actresses at the Lyceum would have been exceedingly shocked at such a frivolous suggestion.

In the midst of all this, there were domestic troubles to be settled. There could be no question of a divorce from Kelly. Ellen had suffered too much already from scandal and wanted no more of it. At the Lyceum she was constantly in the public eye. She had no wish ever to marry again, so a deed of separation was agreed on and they parted. Thankfully, she could turn with a free mind to the work which had come to mean so much to her.

During the previous autumn the American actor Edwin Booth had come to play a season in London. He was four years older than Irving, one of the ten children of Junius Brutus Booth, a great tragedian comparable to Edmund Kean in the opinion of his own countrymen. Edwin had first come to England in 1861 and had played a season in Manchester with a stock company in which Irving had then been a very junior member. He had been deeply impressed with the young American's quiet intellectual acting, the spiritual force of his Hamlet, the thoughtful study of the ambitious soldier who was Macbeth.

Booth's life had known tragedy. His first wife had died early, and now the second Mrs. Booth lay hovering between life and death in a London hotel. Two years before his visit to England, a stagestruck lunatic had fired at him as he played Richard II. The bullets missed him and he never wavered in his performance. In 1865 his career had nearly come to an end when his younger brother, John Wilkes, assassinated Abraham Lincoln as he sat in his box at Ford's Theatre in Washington.

Now, in London Booth had endured a miserable season. The Princess Theatre, where Ellen had acted with Charles Kean, had fallen on bad times. The management was unwilling to spend money on either the company or the scenery for their American guest. In March 1881 Irving generously invited him to play with the Lyceum Company, making the suggestion that they act Othello and Iago on alternate weeks, with Ellen as Desdemona.

Sixty-four years before, in 1817, Booth's father had played Iago to Edmund Kean's Othello. It had been an occasion of deadly rivalry, more like a battle between two heavyweight champions than a dramatic performance by two tragedians. In the second half of the play, Kean played with such blazing ferocity, such savage grandeur, that he completely routed his rival, who hurriedly got out of the rest of the engagement and fled back to America.

No such competition existed between Booth and Irving. Ellen found the American quiet and reserved. "I have never in my life in any country seen such wonderful eyes," she wrote of him. His Othello was gentle and noble. He was very much the star actor, speaking straight out to the audience, unlike Irving, who used and encouraged others to use a natural style of acting. He was very thoughtful and considerate. There was the matter of makeup for Othello, for instance.

"I shall never make you black," he said to Ellen one morning. "When I take your hand, I shall have a corner of my drapery in my hand—that will protect you." She had cause to remember his concern somewhat ruefully the following week when Irving played Othello and she ended up nearly as black as he was.

Behind his reserve, Booth was a keen observer. "Mr. Irving is despotic," he wrote in a vivid account of his experiences. "From first to last he rules the stage with a will of iron, but also with a patience that is marvellous. He sits among his players watching every moment, listening to every word, constantly stopping anyone—Miss Terry as well as the messenger—who do not do exactly right . . . At the Lyceum one sees the perfection of stage discipline and in Mr. Irving the perfection of stage patience."

Ellen's conception of Desdemona was unusual. She did not play her as a pathetic, simple-minded saint, as so many actresses had before her. She saw her as a strong-minded girl who with great moral courage had flouted the conventions in marrying Othello. Shakespeare's heroines, she argued, are not prim or demure, they have no false coquetry. They have purity of heart, and complete frankness when they love. They possess inward freedom and they behave as they feel.

Ellen's greatest triumph, she always thought, was not gained with the audience but in the effect she had on Henry. When she spoke the line, "O good Iago, what shall I do to win my lord again?" she looked up to see him so moved by her tender pathos that, despite his identifying himself with his part, his eyes were soft and luminous with tears. Yet he knew how to turn his emotion to good purpose. He dashed away the tears and blew his nose with such feeling ("So much expression there is, by the way, in blowing the nose on the stage!" comments Ellen) that the audience thought his weakness only a fresh stroke of hypocrisy.

For the first time the critics were in complete accord in praising his performance. He was called daringly Italian, a true compatriot of the Borgias, or rather that devil incarnate, an Englishman Italianate. Ellen wrote in her diary: "One admired him, devil though he was. He was so full of charm, so surely the 'honest' Iago. It was only in the soliloquies that he revealed his devil's nature." And she always remembered the grapes he plucked in the first act and slowly ate. "Virtue! a fig! 'Tis in ourselves that we are thus, or thus!" And he spat out the pips as if each one represented a worthy virtue to be put out of his mouth.

Booth's Iago seemed conventional and ordinary beside this brilliant, startling, picturesque performance, but his Othello was better than Irving's. Henry had fine moments, his speech to the Senate was one of the best things he ever did, the murder scene was deeply moving, thought Ellen, but at other times he raved and raged when he should have been quiet. She would wonder sometimes if his failure was not one of the unspoken bitternesses of his life.

On the last night she watched him slowly fold up his costumes, one by one, laying them in a neat pile, the green and gold robe on the top. "Never again!" he said, half humorously, and very deliberately stretched himself, giving a great sigh of relief. For her it was a sad decision. For with his renunciation died her lovely performance as Desdemona.

The experiment had proved a great popular success. The public came crowding in, eager to make comparisons between the two great actors, even though the stalls had doubled in price. Booth returned to America with a considerable profit in his pocket.

The incessant work of rehearsing daily and acting at night

left Ellen little time for family visiting. Her parents had moved from Camden Town and were living near her in Earl's Court. Ben watched his daughter's career with all his old keen interest.

"Duchess, you could do anything!" he declared after he had seen *Othello*. He admired Irving but wanted to see his Nellie playing bigger and more important parts. "We must have no more of these Ophelias and Desdemonas," he went on. "They're second-fiddle parts, not the parts for you, Duchess."

But Ellen did not agree with him. She was supremely happy. She had none of the vanity and conceit of those who cannot endure to be anything but the leading figure. She would study a small part and play it with as much care and attention as she would an important one.

As for the rest of the family, Marion was making a success of her career, though she was never to achieve the magic and popularity of her sister. Floss had married, and Fred, golden-haired, handsome Fred, just eighteen, had returned from Paris, where he had been finishing his education, and defying his father's wishes, had already started to find himself small parts on the stage.

There was a brief holiday when the season ended, and then for the first time the Lyceum Company went on tour. Such a colossal enterprise had never been known before. Railway transport had vastly improved since the early days when Ellen and Irving had played in provincial stock companies. Scenery, properties, furniture, lighting equipment, costumes, together with the stage staff for nine plays, were loaded into a special train. Irving was determined that the theatrical standards of London which he had done so much to create should be carried to the provincial cities with the actors who had made them.

For the first time, theatregoers in Manchester, Liverpool,

Edinburgh, and the other cities were able to see not just the stars acting with their own everyday stock company but the whole gorgeous spectacle that had enchanted the capital. It was a new and daring experiment and it succeeded beyond anything they had dreamed. It set a standard which others were soon to follow and it netted a considerable profit with which to launch other, even more elaborate productions.

7

Queen of the Stage

THE NEW SEASON at the Lyceum opened on Boxing Day, and early in the New Year Irving took Ellen to see the house he had recently bought at Brook Green, a village near Hammersmith, already nearly swallowed up by the rapid growth of London, but still rural, the tree-lined streets leafy and green.

"The Grange" was two spacious old cottages knocked into one, surrounded by lawns shaded by poplar and chestnut. The house had been redecorated and furnished. Irving had installed a man and wife as gardener and housekeeper and was already indulging his love of dogs. Charley, growing old and very jealous, glared suspiciously at the bulldog and the good-natured Newfoundland who bounded joyfully to greet them.

When Ellen and Irving went out into the gardens, sparkling with frost under a winter sun, he began to tell her enthusiastically how he planned to have them laid out. "Just exactly like one of Hawes Craven's garden settings," she said mischievously.

He smiled at her, acknowledging her shrewd hint that the theatre was never long absent from his mind. "Only that here you can smell the scent of flowers and feel the real warmth and life of the sun," he replied.

The house and garden were an escape from the Lyceum and the rooms in Grafton Street which he could now well afford. Here he could gather his books and pictures and entertain his friends.

Ellen began to tell him of her garden at Harpenden, of the roses and lilacs she had planted, and he listened attentively, watching her face grow soft and tender at the memory.

Their friendship had grown warmer and deeper. At the theatre they were in complete harmony, and a great deal of their leisure was spent together. Invitations to private parties were extended to them both and she usually accompanied him to official receptions. He was a frequent and welcome visitor at Longridge Road and Rose Cottage. Her parents liked him. He had become part of the family.

The affection of Edy and Teddy compensated in some measure for the estrangement from his own sons. On the rare occasions when he saw Harry and Laurence, there was only dislike and constraint between them. This summer he intended to send them to Marlborough, determined that they should have the public-school education he himself had been denied.

Ellen knew, as a woman always knows, that Henry was falling in love with her, but nothing could be done. They were both still married and his wife would never consent to divorce him. So they did not speak of it. In the meantime there was still the theatre, which came first in both their lives.

They went on to discuss *Romeo and Juliet,* the production which was occupying their minds to the exclusion of everything else. "You know," said Irving slowly, "*Hamlet* could be played anywhere on its acting merits. It marches from situation to situation. But *Romeo and Juliet* proceeds from picture to picture . . . It is a dramatic poem rather than a drama and I mean to treat it from that point of view." He smiled at her. "As for you, Nell, you've got to do all you know with it."

She felt the weight of the responsibility. They were both clear-sighted enough to know the risk they were taking. Irving was forty-four, hardly a suitable age for the youthful Romeo. Ellen at thirty-five already felt herself too old for Juliet. It was their last chance to play this most lyrical and tender of all Shakespeare's plays. Henry had at first, she knew, thought of playing Mercutio, but where in all London would he find a Romeo that could match him in experience and ability?

He released Ellen from playing in the evening so she could study Juliet at Rose Cottage in her bedroom overlooking the great park with only the shy deer for company. She read everything that had been written about the play; she racked her brains over the interpretations given by other actresses and wondered afterward if she had not made a mistake. Imagination was what was needed for young, passionate Juliet, not close study. Sometimes she thought she had never played it so well as when she rehearsed it to herself in the stalactite caverns of the Regents Park Colosseum.

The play, like so much of Shakespeare, had suffered cruel mutilation in past centuries at the hands of unscrupulous actors and managers, even being given a happy ending. Irving restored much of the original text and defied tradition by refusing to produce it as a pretty, romantic tale of two hapless lovers. In-

COURTESY OF ROGER MANVELL

Ellen as Juliet, 1882

stead, he brought to vivid life a Verona torn by the feuds of vicious gangsters, a city of dark, dangerous streets where enemies lurked, set against a background of Renaissance splendor. His mastery of the crowd scenes was remarkable. He created a series of magnificent stage pictures: Romeo in his green cloak and doublet, with an oleander sprig in his crimson cap, coming into the hall of the Capulets with its azalea trees and silver brocade hangings; the brawling young men with their violent duels; the procession of maidens scattering flowers who came to take Juliet to her wedding; the final reconciliation of the two families at the tomb of the lovers.

The critics, dumfounded by the beauty of the production, nevertheless damned the two chief players with faint praise. But there were many in the audience who remembered all their lives Juliet's honey-sweet voice filled with the agony of a grief-stricken child; the flaming intensity of Romeo's first glance at her, drawing her eyes to his as by the spell of a mesmerist; the blind, wildcat fury with which he hurled himself at Tybalt after Mercutio's death; the tragic "parrot" scream of the old Nurse at finding her darling "dead" on her marriage morn.

Ellen and Irving, severely critical of their own performances, did their utmost to sustain each other. "Beautiful as Portia was," he wrote to her after the dress rehearsal, "Juliet leaves her far far behind. Never has anybody acted more exquisitely the part of the performance I saw from the front. 'Hie to high fortune' and 'where spirits resort' were simply incomparable . . . Your mother looked very radiant last night. I told her how proud she should be, and she was." He added a rueful postscript: "I have determined not to see a paper for a week—I know they'll cut me up and I don't like it."

Ellen judged Irving's performance as pitilessly as she judged her own. Self-criticism, she considered, was an essential part of an actor's growth in his art. "I am not going to say that Henry's Romeo was good," she wrote in her diary. "What I do say is that some bits of it were as good as anything he ever did . . . At the opening of the Apothecary Scene when Balthasar comes to tell Romeo of Juliet's supposed death, Henry was marvellous.

Then she is well and nothing can be ill;
Her body sleeps in Capulet's monument.

It was during the silence after these two lines that Henry had one of those sublime moments which an actor only achieves once or twice in his life." There was absolutely no movement, but his face grew whiter and whiter and the audience knew what was going on in his soul.

When he was attacked, she flew loyally to his defense. "Why is Irving playing Romeo?" asked Henry Labouchère, the eminent journalist and politician, one night. "I don't doubt his intellectuality, you know. But as Romeo he reminds me of a pig who has been taught to play the fiddle. He does it cleverly but he would be better employed in squealing." Furious at the jibe, she replied icily: "I am sorry you don't realise that the worst thing Henry Irving could do would be better than the best of anyone else."

It was during the run of *Romeo and Juliet* that Sally Holland came to be Ellen's dresser, and she remained with her throughout the Lyceum years. She was extremely methodical where Ellen was untidy. She never became flustered and each costume was freshly pressed every day. She adored her mistress and at this time, when Ellen was thin as a beanpole and worried about it, she used to say encouragingly, "Beautiful and fat tonight, dear," as she laced her into her dress.

Neither Irving nor Ellen indulged in luxurious star dressing rooms. Their rooms were both situated on the opposite prompt side—that is on the right-hand side of the stage, up a small flight of stairs, whereas the rest of the company dressed on the prompt side.

Every night Sally would arrive early, laying down the square of white drugget on the floor to protect the beautiful costumes. Then she would set out the pans of color powders, which would be applied with a damp sponge. Greasepaint had already been invented by the Bavarian opera singer Max Leichner, but Ellen preferred the fullers earth and rice powder of her youth, and the harsh effect of the dry paint, which had made many an actress's face raddled and coarse, never seemed to have the slightest ill effect on her thick, creamy, magnolia-like skin. A hare's-foot and a pot of rouge completed the simple preparations.

Gas lamps on adjustable brackets surrounded the mirror. There was a comfortable armchair, usually occupied by visitors. Photographs of the children and of theatrical friends, with cables and messages of good wishes stuck behind pictures or pinned to the walls, were the only decoration, except for the flowers that arrived nightly from dozens of admirers. On the hundredth performance of *Romeo and Juliet,* she was deeply touched by a bouquet sent as a mark of respect and esteem from the "Gasmen of the Lyceum Theatre."

That night Irving gave another supper party on the stage, the orchestra pit banked with flowers, so that the guests seemed to look out on a moonlit garden. Sarah Bernhardt had been in the audience and she came hurrying backstage to put her arms around Ellen, pouring out praises half in English, half in French. "She was transparent as an azalea, only more so," wrote Ellen. "Smoke from a burning paper describes her more nearly!" She had a tremendous and ungrudging admiration for the great French actress.

After supper, Irving gave the first intimation that the following year he would be taking the company to America. It was received with rounds of applause. Whatever Ellen and he felt about the play and whatever the critics had said, the public was wildly enthusiastic. Together, they were riding the crest of the wave.

There were also moments of laughter. Coming down the stairs one night dressed to go home, they saw a small girl sitting forlornly on the lowest step. Irving, who was always kind to children, stopped and peered down at her from behind his eyeglasses. "What are you doing here, my dear?"

"Waiting for Mother, sir."

"Are you acting in the theatre?"

"Yes, sir."

"And what part do you take?"

Gazing up at them with huge eyes, Sally Holland's very small daughter said solemnly, "Please, sir, I'm a water carrier, then I'm a page, and then I'm a virgin."

They collapsed on the stairs, laughing until they cried.

Ellen, looking back in later years, remembered how many young men who afterward reached a great position in the theatre had their first experience and learned their first lessons in stagecraft at the Lyceum. There had been Arthur Wing

Pinero, who had played Rosencrantz in *Hamlet* and Roderigo in *Othello* among other parts, and whose first one-act plays, *Daisy's Escape* and *Bygones,* were produced by Irving, with the author himself in the lead. He was to achieve fame with *Trelawney of the Wells, The Second Mrs. Tanqueray,* and *The Magistrate* among others, but he never forgot the lessons in dramatic technique, in building a situation into a climax, that he learned from the Guv'nor.

There was George Alexander, a young actor they had seen on tour in Edinburgh and brought back to play Paris in *Romeo and Juliet,* and John Martin Harvey, an awestruck youngster, walking on at twenty-five shillings a week. Both of them were later to found their own companies.

Irving could be brusque with these young men, but he would work tirelessly teaching them, sometimes too much so in Ellen's opinion. They were so impressed with him that they would strive to turn themselves into copies of him—he who was unique, but the training they received was invaluable.

Irving often asked her to do the same for the young actresses, but though she was always kind and encouraging, she was not a born teacher as he was. She did feel, however, that she was a useful buffer between the Guv'nor and the rest of the company. They all came to her, sometimes even Bram Stoker and Loveday, with what they dare not say to him, knowing full well that he would listen to her and even allow himself to be persuaded, though never against his own judgment.

Frank Benson was another of these young men. He had come down from Oxford quite certain that he knew everything about the art of acting. Irving and Ellen had been greatly impressed by his playing of Clytemnestra in an undergraduate performance of the *Agamemnon* of Aeschylus.

When George Alexander left the cast to join the Kendals at the St. James's Theatre, Benson was given his first chance as Paris, an opportunity for which any ambitious young professional actor would have given a great deal. The handsome boy, who had never gone through the hard grind of a stock company, never starved in a dreary garret or waited hours to change trains on a freezing railway station, arrived at the stage door flushed with his amateur successes, seeing himself as a torch-bearer, a new kind of actor combining scholarship and numerous academic theories with a splendid physique. He was to be taught a very sharp lesson.

"So here you are at last," said Mr. Allen, the prompter, impatiently, before he even had a chance to open his mouth. "You're taking Mr. Alexander's place, I understand. You're jolly lucky to get the chance. Now get over there. We'll just run through your part before you meet the company."

In a very few days, pretensions and theories were all stripped away. The brisk professionalism of the other players confused him. He stumbled through his moves, and his lines flew out of his head. The one thing left to him was a firm belief in his skill as a swordsman. There, at any rate, he knew himself far better than anyone at the Lyceum, even the chief himself.

Lying stretched on the tomb, Ellen smiled as she watched him face up to Romeo in the last duel. He carefully arranged himself in the correct position, completely confident of his superior ability. Irving took in the situation at a glance. He ignored the beautiful stance and fiercely attacked the astonished young man. There was a preliminary clash of swords, then he hit him hard over the knuckles with his foil, prodded him in the stomach with his knee, sent his rapier flying out of his hand, and muttering, "Die—me boy—die," elbowed him into the mouth of the tomb and forced him to the ground. All the brilliant passages of the fencing school had been lost in the furious onslaught of a cut-and-thrust theatrical duel.

Somewhat stunned, Benson still had one theory to which he clung. Makeup, he had been told, spoiled facial expression. To the horror of the actors with whom he shared a dressing room, he went down to dress rehearsal with his handsome features quite clean of paint.

When he came off after his first scene, a furious Bram Stoker met him in the wings. "What's wrong with you, for heaven's sake? Your face looks dirty. Are you sweating with fright or what is it?"

It was a hot night, explained Benson, and he had a theory . . .

"Forget your theories!" exploded Stoker. "Go and get yourself made up like everyone else!"

Shaken and humbled, Benson got through the first night somehow. He was greatly cheered by the little note Ellen sent around to his dressing room: "Well done for first done."

Out of kindness of heart, and recognizing the boy's inner earnestness and will to improve, she interceded with Irving to allow him to watch the play from the wings. "Only make your notes afterwards, *not* during the play," she begged him.

Night after night he sat there drinking it in and once had the daring to approach Irving as he waited for his entrance. "A very beautiful part, that of Romeo," he remarked as one great man to another.

"Yes," snapped Irving, "and the odd thing about it is that every damn young fool who's been on the stage two minutes thinks he can play it." It was a chilling rebuff. Suddenly the young man was giddily aware of the gulf that loomed between academic theory and the needs of the professional theatre.

Old Mrs. Stirling, who had acted with Macready and had been called out of retirement to play the Nurse, gave him a piece of sound advice: "You will never be an actor until you have learned to get through your part though the snow comes through the roof; with an audience of only two or three drunks, who are not listening; while sparrows twitter and flitter round the auditorium before settling to roost in the flies; while rats trot across the footlights with your pet powder-puff in their mouths; when you have not had a square meal for a month and will probably get no salary on Saturday; when you are sent on for a part of two or three hundred lines with one night's study, and no proper rehearsal."

These were the things he never forgot when he came to form his own company and as Sir Frank Benson to make theatrical history all over England, Canada, and South Africa.

"Thank you very much for writing me a word of encouragement," he wrote to Ellen. "I feel doubly grateful to you and Mr. Irving for the light you shed from the lamp of art on life now that I begin to understand the labour and weariness the process of trimming the lamp entails."

The last new production before they went to America was *Much Ado about Nothing*. Ellen was born to play Beatrice. Shakespeare's lines might have been written with her in mind. "For out of question," says Don Pedro to Beatrice, "you were born in a merry hour."

"No, sure, my lord," is her gay reply. "My mother cried, but then there was a star danced and under that was I born."

Flashingly witty, merry, mocking, yet infinitely tender, she

THE NEW YORK PUBLIC LIBRARY PICTURE COLLECTION

Ellen as Beatrice. The inscription is in her own hand

was perhaps nearer to her real self there than in any other part, and ever since Leeds when she had appeared in it with Charles Kelly, she had longed to play it again. In Benedick, Irving achieved a perfect balance between dry humor and a romantic gallantry. Their scenes together were a delight.

Johnston Forbes-Robertson, who had played with her when she first came back to the theatre, was a sensitive Claudio, and Terriss was a gallant Don Pedro, as impulsive as ever, and so amusingly outrageous that no one, not even Irving, could be angry with him. One morning he turned up at rehearsal so very late that for once, Ellen noted, Henry spoke quite sharply to him.

"I think you'll be sorry you've spoken to me like this, Guv'nor," replied Terriss sadly.

"Now, no hanky-panky tricks, Terriss."

"Tricks, Guv'nor! I think you'll regret having said that when you hear that my poor mother passed away early this morning." And the tears stood in his eyes.

Irving, with quick sympathy, gave him the day off.

A week or so later, he and Ellen were peering at the audience through a slit in the canvas before the curtain went up, and Terriss said gaily, "See that dear old woman sitting in the fourth row of the stalls? That's my mother"—quite forgetting that he had killed her off!

Teddy, sitting in the stage box, remembered the first night of *Much Ado about Nothing* for the rest of his life: the gaiety, the brilliance, his mother sweeping down toward him in the final dance with everyone applauding, the superb church scene with real pillars, a canopied roof of red plush from which hung golden lamps, the great altar with the stained-glass windows behind it.

It was over that scene that Ellen had her first quarrel with Irving. For the sake of dramatic emphasis he suggested, as other producers had done before him, that they end the scene with a repeat of Beatrice's line: "Benedick, kill Claudio!" to which he would reply: "As sure as I'm alive, I will."

"You can't do it. It's not Shakespeare," she argued passionately. "It's vandalism. Every scholar will attack you for it."

They fought over it for a week. Stubbornly, she refused to say the line. Then one day Henry said, "Now I think it about time to rehearse this scene as we are actually going to play it, so, Miss Terry, we must please have the gag."

She did not like to show insubordination before the company, so with a gulp she managed to obey, but she burst into tears. Henry was sympathetic but would not budge. She went home in a terrible state of mind, strongly tempted to give up her part. Then, in a calmer mood, she reflected that for the one thing she did not like doing at the Lyceum there would probably be a hundred things she would dislike doing in another theatre. So she agreed to do as he wished, under protest. And then of course, in the brilliance of the acting, neither the critics nor the scholars even noticed it, and Henry said nothing, only looked maddeningly triumphant.

The play ran from October till June of 1883 to crowded houses and then was withdrawn so that the plays they were taking to America could be revived. After the huge success of *Much Ado about Nothing,* they of course left London in a blaze of glory. On the last night of the season the theatre was packed from floor to ceiling and the applause was deafening. The whole company gathered on the stage to sing *Auld Lang Syne* with the audience. For Ellen and Irving, standing hand in hand, it was a triumphant moment.

A few months earlier, Edward, Prince of Wales, had been

entertained at a supper on the stage. Through Gladstone, now Prime Minister, had come hints of a knighthood, which Irving took pains to indicate that he would not accept, but all the same it was gratifying evidence that his efforts to raise actors to the position held by artists in other fields had not gone unnoticed.

Before leaving London, Irving was given a farewell banquet by five hundred distinguished members of various professions. In those days it was men only at such a gathering, but after dinner Ellen appeared on the balcony of the hall to the loudest applause of the evening.

"A fairer vision than Ellen Terry, then at the zenith of her loveliness, cannot be imagined," wrote Graham Robertson, the artist, one of her young admirers. "She shone with no shallow sparkle or glitter, but with a steady radiance that filled the room, and had the peculiar quality of making everybody else invisible."

There still remained a short provincial tour, and Ellen, wretched at the thought of parting with her children, with the bullfinch and the parrot and all that meant home at Longridge Road, took Teddy and Edy with her for these last few weeks.

In Glasgow they were invited by Sir William Pearce to visit his palatial yacht, the *Lady Torfrida,* lying in the river Clyde. They embarked in the skiff after the play, nearly at midnight. It was black and stormy, the wind and the rain lashed down, and their path across the water was lit with lurid blue flares. They were not dismayed, Irving because he felt he bore a charmed life, having once missed being blown up, and Ellen because she loved any kind of adventure. Despite the fact that Sir William himself was their steersman, they very nearly missed the ship and came close to drowning.

The next morning, in glittering sunshine sailing down the

river, they saw a rocky island rising out of the blue-gray waters of the Firth of Clyde. The captain gave orders for a small signal cannon to be fired, and thousands of gulls swept off the rock into the sky, swarming and circling above it, their screams mingling with the shrill song of the wind in the rigging.

"That's Ailsa Craig," said Sir William.

"What a wonderful stage name!" exclaimed Ellen. "A pity you can't have it, Ted, I shall give it to Edy instead."

The decision made on impulse was carried out. Later, when the children were formally christened and confirmed, Irving standing as godfather, Edy became Edith Ailsa Craig and Teddy became Edward Gordon Craig, a name which one day he would make world famous.

On October 11 Ellen and Irving sailed from Liverpool on the *Britannic*. Behind them in London they left an assured reputation. Apart from the Bancrofts at the Haymarket and the Kendals at the St. James, there was no management presenting productions of equal quality to theirs. No one else had arisen to challenge their supremacy. Now together they were preparing to risk their names on the other side of the Atlantic in a country which had sometimes in the past shown itself hostile to English actors.

There is a tide in the affairs of men
Which, taken at the flood, leads on to fortune.

It was a hazardous and costly enterprise, but it had always been Irving's way to win or lose all, and at least he and Ellen were together.

8

The Land across the Atlantic

AMERICA, THE COUNTRY where Macready had been hooted from the stage, where the press had savaged Edmund Kean and was so severely critical that an actor's career could be broken in a day, where the women wore red-flannel shirts and carried bowie knives and one could be shot up by bandits or sandbagged in the streets . . . For years Ellen had been hearing tales like these, and now she found out it was not like that at all.

By 1883 the United States supported a native theatre quite as prosperous, cultured, and rich in actors and actresses as that in Great Britain. They would be playing to a highly intelligent public coolly judging them against the talents of their own fine artists. But never before had an actor-manager brought from England a complete company with scenery, costumes, and properties for nine productions of romantic and Shakespearean plays.

"We were the first and we were pioneers and we were *new*," wrote Ellen. "To be *new* is everything in America."

She was an excellent sailor and had enjoyed the voyage despite the buffeting of the sea. Everything had been done for their comfort. She had two cabins for her sole use, and a corner of the saloon had been screened off as a private sitting room. Miss Harries had come with her as companion. And then there was Fussie.

The little fox terrier had been a gift from Fred Archer. The boy who had delivered the milk and brought the vegetables at Harpenden had fulfilled his ambitions. He was England's most famous jockey. Still thin as a herring, for he starved himself to keep his weight down, he had won 241 races the previous year, including the Derby, the St. Leger, the Oaks, and the Grand Prix.

She had met him again on a visit to Newmarket, the center of the racing world, and he had promised her one of the terriers he bred himself. "I'll send you a dog, Miss Terry," he said, "that won't be any trouble. He's got a very good head, a first-rate tail stuck in splendidly, but his legs are too long. He'd follow you to America!"

Fussie had arrived at the Lyceum one afternoon and had settled in at once. He had his own piece of carpet which he dragged himself if no one carried it for him; he became firm friends with Charley and right from the start was passionately attached to Irving. More often than not, even in the first few weeks, Ellen would go into his dressing room to find both dogs curled up in the two available chairs and Henry standing to put on his makeup rather than disturb them.

The *Britannic* anchored off Staten Island in the early hours of October 21. A boatload of reporters met them as soon as they were dressed. They peppered Ellen with questions.

"What are your favorite characters, Miss Terry?"

"Oh, I don't know," she said, her eyes roving over this new land, the broad river, the gay wooden villas on the shore, the brown hills. "I love nearly all I play . . . I like comedy best, Portia, Beatrice . . ."

"You prefer to cast your future with the Lyceum Company?"

"Yes, certainly," was the quick reply. "I am devoted to the Lyceum and to Mr. Irving. No one admires him more than I do; no one knows better, I think, how much he has done for our art; no one dreams of how much more he will yet do if he is spared."

In England one was always aware of the poetry of the past, thought Ellen, as the boat took them ashore, but here it was the poetry of the present, gigantic, colossal. When she looked out over the marvelous harbor with its multitudes of steamboats, its wharf upon wharf, and the tall Statue of Liberty dominating the noise and bustle of the sea traffic, she nearly cried, it was so beautiful. Then there was Brooklyn Bridge hung up high in the air like a vast spider's web.

They opened on October 29 at the Star Theatre with *The Bells.* Ellen was in a box with Gilbert Coleridge, an old friend, son of the Lord Chief Justice, who was on a visit to the States. That evening New York was drowned in a deluge of rain. Those who fought their way through the mud-splashed streets and gurgling gutters received the first act in a stony silence.

Ellen, nerves on edge, sent Coleridge backstage. He found Henry pacing up and down his dressing room like a caged lion. "It's a frost," he exclaimed. "I'm doing my best but these Yankees are icebergs, blocks and stones . . . I might as well play to a churchyard!"

In the second act the ice began to thaw. And at the fall of the curtain the applause was deafening. Afterward, when Coleridge and Irving escorted Ellen back to her hotel, she broke into a dance of sheer joy at their success. Arm in arm, to the astonishment of passers-by, the trio danced their way to the steps of the hotel.

The next night she made her debut as Henrietta Maria in *Charles I.* "Command yourself! This is the time to show you can act," she said sternly to herself. But, as so often, she felt she had played badly and cried far too much, but the audience took her to their hearts. The Americans fell in love with her, as she did with their beautiful country. "A wonderful land," she called it, "a land of sunshine and light, of happiness, of faith in the future!"

Her first performance in Shakespeare was as Portia and she could not help but be pleased at her reception. *Hamlet* was reserved for Philadelphia. It was the most old-world place she had seen in America with its red-brick sidewalks, the trees in the streets, the low houses with their marble cuffs and collars, the quaint Quaker atmosphere.

At the Chestnut Street Theatre, a fastidious intellectual audience sat silent for the first two acts, uncertain of this quiet, natural acting, of a Hamlet who seemed to throw away his best lines, an Ophelia who was an innocent, bewildered child, so different from the ranting artificialities to which they had become accustomed. The play scene swept them off their feet. They yelled for Ellen and Irving, but it was their firm rule never to take curtain calls between acts. The reception at the end was all the more outstanding.

Boston, Baltimore, Chicago, St. Louis, Cincinnati, Columbus, and Washington—they played them all, traveling in a private train with two sixty-foot boxcars and a huge gondola carrying scenery, properties, and a hundred and fifty stage baskets. The Irving troupe became familiar figures at far-flung railway depots: Ellen with her top coat cut in an unusual and dashing style, an aureole of golden hair escaping from under her brown feathered hat, a loose, flame-colored scarf tied at her throat, not fashionable but timelessly elegant and graceful. The Guv'nor, with his astrakhan coat and wide-brimmed felt hat, eyeglasses perched on aquiline nose, carrying the elderly Charley in his arms; Terriss in fur coat and cap, breezy and handsome, every young girl's ideal Englishman; old Howe with the rosy face and well-cut tweeds of the typical British country gentleman.

Their journey from Boston to Baltimore was made in a blizzard. Since they were expected to play on Christmas Day, Irving entertained his company to supper on the train, and while they feasted on oyster pies, roast beef, and cream jellies, their train was being towed on rafts down the Harlem River from Jersey City. They reached Baltimore with only four hours to spare, but somehow the scenery was unpacked and set up, Sally Holland was busily ironing costumes, and the company rehearsed still in topcoats, hats, and gloves.

The audience, who had struggled through snowdrifts twelve feet high to reach the theatre, was small but enthusiastic, and afterward in her hotel room Ellen hung up holly and mistletoe and triumphantly produced a Christmas pudding made by her mother which she had brought out from England.

The year 1884 opened with one of the worst winters America

had experienced. The storms were terrifying. Lake Michigan was frozen over and cattle for Chicago's stockyards were frozen to death in the freight trains. But Ellen and Irving went for long sleigh rides along the ice-covered banks, exhilarated by the sparkling frosty air, and she found to her astonishment that Chicago, far from being the barbarous city she had imagined, gave them one of the most responsive audiences of the tour.

In February, during a few days' holiday between journeys, Ellen saw Niagara Falls. Her first impression was that they were more wonderful than beautiful, fascinating in size and color but frightening. The irrepressible Terriss, trying to get a closer view, slipped and very nearly lost his life. That night, appearing as Bassanio, he shrugged his shoulders and winked at her, whispering, "Nearly gone, dear, but not quite. Bill's luck!"

Everywhere they went, they were entertained. In Brooklyn they met the great revivalist preacher, Henry Ward Beecher, who broke a lifelong rule and went to the theatre to see *Louis XI*. The next day Ellen and Irving lunched with him and his wife, and he brought out his collection of jewels, asking her to pick out one for herself. The aquamarine she selected he had magnificently set in the style of a Venetian ring for her to wear as Portia.

It was at Brooklyn, too, that there was a moment of unrehearsed comedy. When Charles I was taking his last tragic farewell of his Queen, Fussie so far forgot himself as to make an unexpected appearance. The children who were playing Princess Mary and Prince Henry did not even smile, and the audience remained solemn. But Ellen and Henry nearly went into hysterics at the sight of Fussie rolling over on his back, all four paws waving in the air, whimpering an abject apology. It was the children who had the good sense to take him up to the window at the back, where he cowered between them while they suppressed their giggles and brought the play to a proper conclusion.

In Washington President Chester Arthur not only paid a state visit to the theatre to see *Louis XI* and *The Belle's Stratagem* but invited them to dine with him at the White House. After all the other guests had departed, he kept them talking until the early hours of the morning.

In April the tour came to an end with *Much Ado about Nothing* on a return visit to New York. It was Ellen's greatest triumph. "She permeates the railing of Beatrice with an indescribable charm of mischievous sweetness," said the *Tribune*. So successful had the venture proved that in his farewell speech Irving promised to return in the autumn. They sailed at the end of April, in high spirits and in good fighting fettle for a new London production. Ellen, who had received rave reviews wherever she went, was longing to see the children: Edy, who had been sent as a boarder to Miss Cole's School at Earl's Court, and Teddy, who for the first time had left home to go to a private school at Tunbridge Wells in Kent.

Irving had raised her salary to two hundred pounds a week. These were happy, glorious days. The future had never looked more brilliant.

Boos and hisses from their faithful pit and gallery, catcalls when Irving made the mistake of turning on the audience angrily in his first-night speech—it was a hateful experience. An unhappy fate seemed to have dogged the carefully produced *Twelfth Night*. The evening of July 8 was hot and sultry.

The prim Victorian audience did not relish the rowdy comedy of Sir Toby Belch and Sir Andrew Aguecheek nor did they understand Irving's dignified Malvolio. Ellen, who should have been an exquisite Viola, was so sick and faint with the agony of a poisoned thumb that she was forced to play most of her scenes sitting down with her arm in a sling.

And yet Teddy, who was twelve that year, remembered the play vividly all his life and the deep impression Henry made on him, playing not the usual conceited buffoon but a Malvolio who was solemnly comic, distinguished, and tragic in the final act, imprisoned in a dark room and mocked by Feste, the clown.

Handsome Fred Terry had been engaged to play Sebastian—so like Ellen that they were a perfect brother and sister—but unfortunately after a few nights she was out of the cast. Dr. Stoker, Bram's brother, who was in the audience one evening, came hurrying backstage and lanced what she thought was a bad blister but was actually a vicious bite from a horse fly. But for his prompt action, she might have lost her arm. The next day and for many weeks afterward she was so ill with blood poisoning that Irving, distraught with anxiety, had straw laid down in the road outside the house to deaden the clip-clop of the horses and the noisy rattle of the carriages passing by.

Her sister Marion took her place at the Lyceum, but Ellen was still scarcely recovered by the time the company sailed on the *Parisian* for Canada, where they were to open in Quebec on September 30. After a brave start she collapsed once more and was forced to remain in Montreal while the company went on without her. She rejoined them in Toronto, where she had her first experience of tobogganing, a marvelous sensation. She felt as if she were flying through the freezing air.

They crossed the border to find America in the throes of a Presidential election, but it made little difference to their success. Quite recovered, Ellen was at last able to do full justice to Viola, and the play that had failed in London was one of the most popular across the seas. On her finger she wore a ring that Henry had given her on the first night, a dark blue stone surrounded with diamonds which had once belonged to Madame Vestris, the famous actress and singer.

The two American tours were so close together that, looking back, Ellen would find her memories of them intermingling. Yet there were moments that stood out as vividly as pictures. On one of the endless train journeys she sat studying Henry's face, as she often did, and, struck by a curious look, half puzzled, half despairing, she asked him what he was thinking about.

"I was thinking," he answered slowly, "how strange it is that I should have made the reputation I have as an actor with nothing to help me. My legs, my voice—everything has been against me. For an actor who can't walk, can't talk, and has no face to speak of, I've done pretty well."

With a warm rush of affection, Ellen looked at the splendid head, the wonderfully expressive hands, all the strange fascination that was so much part of him, and smiled to herself. How little he knew!

During the last two years she had seen so little of the children that in a sudden burst of loneliness and homesickness she sent a cable to England to ask Stephen Coleridge, brother of Gilbert and a dear friend, to bring one of them over in time for Christmas. Coleridge arrived with an excited Teddy on December 23 at Pittsburgh, the city which had been called "hell with the lid off" but which Ellen found fierily beautiful, especially at night, when its furnaces turned it into a city of flame.

Henry had planned a festive supper for his company, but the hotel let him down sadly. The meal began with burned hare soup and went on from bad to worse. "It seems to me," he said dryly, "that we're not going to get anything to eat at all, but we'll make up for it by drinking." He had taken the precaution of bringing his own wine with him from England.

"Never mind," said Ellen gaily. "There's always the pudding that Ted has brought us from England." It came in flaming with brandy and looking superb. Henry took the first mouthful. "Very odd," he remarked carefully. "But I think this is a camphor pudding." And it was! Ellen's maid in England had packed it in the basket with her furs! It reeked of camphor balls.

They dined off Henry's wine and witty conversation. One of the children of the company presented Ellen with a silver tea service from the gentlemen of the Lyceum, reciting a set of pretty verses.

"To offer you this little gift,
Dear Portia, now we crave your leave,
And let it have the grace to lift
Our hearts to you this Christmas Eve."

Deeply touched, she could only stammer a few words of thanks through her tears.

She had recovered all her gaiety and high spirits. On the long journey from Chicago, when the train stopped for a twenty-minute wait, she was out on the platform, pulling Teddy across the frozen snow on his shiny sled, pretending to be a horse, shouting with laughter, her hair tumbled like a schoolgirl, every bit as young in spirit as her son, while Henry watched her, smiling from the steps of the railway car.

Inevitably it was the dogs who provided moments of comedy. Henry took Fussie for a ride on the El to the amazement of the New Yorkers. The papers drew caricatures of a tiny Ellen with a Fussie the size of an elephant or a very big Ellen with a very small terrier. He raced beside the carriage when they crossed Brooklyn Bridge, looking in winter like a gigantic trellis dazzling with snow and ice, incredible as a dream.

American hotels did not look kindly on dogs, and Henry would walk straight out if objections were raised. Once, when very tired, he let Fussie go to the stables and sent Walter, his dresser, to look after him, but the next morning he tackled the hotel manager. "Yours is a very old-fashioned hotel, isn't it?"

"Yes, sir, very ancient."

"I'm afraid you don't like animals."

"In their proper place, sir."

"A pity," remarked Henry quietly, "because you happen to be overrun with rats."

"Sir, you must be mistaken," exclaimed the horrified manager.

"Well, I couldn't pass another night here without my dog, but I suppose there are other hotels . . ."

"If it will be any comfort to you to have your dog, do by all means," replied the manager coldly, "but he'll catch no rats here."

"I'll be on the safe side," said Henry calmly.

That night Fussie feasted on terrapin and chicken and other delicacies in his private sitting room. The way to Fussie's heart was through his stomach, and he was already beginning to desert Ellen for Irving, the generous bestower of tidbits.

In Boston the incredible happened. Henry, who was never ill, was out of the cast for a few days with rheumatism in his leg so painful that he was unable to stand. It caused something like panic in the company. George Alexander, who had replaced Terriss on this tour, played Benedick at a few hours' notice. But it was Ellen who saved the situation. As Beatrice she bore the burden on her shoulders and rose to the occasion magnificently. The next night, as Portia, with old Tom Mead struggling bravely with the part of Shylock, she again aroused the audience to wild enthusiasm.

It was not only the young men who worshipped her. The girls and women of America were all her slaves. She was guest of honor at the Papyrus Club and they crowded around her, hemming her in, mad with curiosity, to ask question after question, to look closer at her unusual dress with its red, loosely folded sash. She looked like some eighteenth-century portrait, her delicate complexion catching a rosy reflection from the satin scarf tied in a bow at her throat, her charming face seemingly modeled on that of some Pre-Raphaelite saint.

Teddy was having the time of his life. He detested school, and here in America, as Ellen's son, he was fussed over and made much of. To please her, Irving had given him the little part of Joey, the gardener's boy, in *Eugene Aram*. In Chicago, just before his thirteenth birthday, he made his first appearance in a speaking part and was sure that what he wanted more than anything was to be an actor. Like his mother, he admired and loved Irving, "who proved to be so much to me, to my work and to my aims," he wrote in later life, "proved as kind as a father—maybe (as he was very human) he knew what it might feel like having no father."

He walked on in the other plays and loved every minute of

THE NEW YORK PUBLIC LIBRARY PICTURE COLLECTION

Henry Irving as the Vicar and Ellen as Olivia

it. "His eyes are full of sparkle, his smile is a ripple over his face and his laughter is as cheery and natural as a bird's song," wrote a critic. "He has the instinct and the soul of art in him. Already the theatre is his home." Ellen thought that the nicest press notice she had ever read.

She was very proud, too, that both Irving and she gained not only the friendship but the approval of Dr. Horace Howard Furness, America's great Shakespearean scholar, whose Variorum Shakespeare edition Henry thought the best of all, the "one that counts."

The tour came to an end in April. It had proved extremely profitable but, more than that, it had added enormous prestige to Ellen and Irving. They had shown that they could hold audiences not only in England but throughout the United States and Canada. In the future, surely nothing would prove to be impossible.

Ellen came back to her own country and to sorrow at the loss of friends. Charles Reade, who had been like a second father to her, had died while she was in America. One morning shortly after her return, a beautiful but untidy young woman called at Longridge Road. "Miss Terry, would you come quickly?" she said urgently. "Mr. Wardell is very ill and wants to see you." They went at once by cab to the very poor lodgings where Charles Kelly lay dying. He had longed to see her again and she remained sitting beside him, holding his hand, until he died. She left in tears, distressed because these last years, absorbed in her busy, happy life, she had not even thought of the man she had married. She paid his debts and provided for his dependents with a feeling that she had never been quite fair to him.

She was thirty-eight, a widow now, but the demands of the

theatre left little time to mourn for him. In a month *Olivia* was to be revived, a production Irving could safely leave to Ellen and Terriss. It was almost a family play, she thought, with Edy and Teddy walking on and Marion as her understudy. It was the most comfortable first night she had ever had at the Lyceum.

The only one who seemed out of the cozy picture was Irving himself as Goldsmith's saintly Dr. Primrose, the Vicar of Wakefield. It was Edy, fifteen now and a very sharp critic, who put her finger on what was wrong. "Don't go on like that, Henry," Edy said one morning at rehearsal. She had never been in the least afraid of him. "You're not Mathias in *The Bells*. Why don't you talk as you do to me and Teddy? At home you are the Vicar." Ellen trembled for her outspoken child, but he was not offended. Instead, he took her advice and on the first night he walked on and *was* the simple lovable old clergyman, just as he was the Prince in *Hamlet* or the king in *Charles I*.

9

Bright Star

THE LEGEND OF FAUST and his unholy pact with the Devil had always fascinated Irving, and now W. G. Wills had produced a workable acting version for him from Goethe's massive masterpiece. In August he swept Ellen off to Germany in search of local color. Included in the party were Edy and Teddy, together with two dear friends of Ellen's, Joe and Alice Comyns Carr. Joe was linked with the aesthetic movement, a close friend of the artists Burne-Jones and John Sargent, and beginning to be known as a playwright. His wife, Alice, was interested in helping to design the costumes.

The imperial city of Nuremberg, which went back at least to the year 1240, was their first stop. The children made the fascinating discovery that Tannhäuser, Hans Sachs, the shoemaker-poet, and the Mastersingers were not just characters in Wagner's operas but had once walked in these same ancient Gothic streets. Commanded by Henry, the whole party spent enchanted hours rummaging through antique shops and markets, buying up properties of every kind and shape and sending them back in crates to the Lyceum.

Irving spent lavishly, and the city welcomed the eccentric English visitors with rapture. An orchestra serenaded them under their hotel windows one morning. Ellen went rapping with her umbrella at the great gate of the castle when it was closed for the day and as if by magic it opened at her touch and she was shown through the castle. One night there was a tremendous fire that lit up the whole sky, and Henry, called to watch from Ellen's window, was heard to murmur, "If only we could put that on at the Lyceum!"

They moved on to Rothenburg, finding it easy to believe in the old legend in this walled medieval city with its gray stone fountains scarlet with geraniums, its painted wooden houses, and the swans floating on the waters of the river Tauber. The watchman's call still echoed through the streets at nightfall as it had for centuries.

Faust was produced on December 19, 1885, with all the lavish pictorial effects we might see today in an epic film. There were angelic visions, descents into a sulfurous inferno, magical appearances, and trap-door disappearances. The critics called it claptrap, but all the same Margaret became one of Ellen's favorite parts, even though she did not think the lines as poetic as those of *Charles I*. She was proud of learning how to use a spinning wheel so as to give the right touch of reality, and Alice's fifteenth-century costumes were striking enough to be copied by Madame Nellie Melba, the prima donna, when next she sang in Gounod's opera.

THE NEW YORK PUBLIC LIBRARY PICTURE COLLECTION

Ellen as Marguerite

George Alexander was a splendidly romantic Faust, and though she did not care for Henry's Mephistopheles as much as she had for other roles, he had marvelous moments, she admitted.

When he wrote in the student's book, "Ye shall be as gods, knowing good and evil," he seemed suddenly and uncannily to become a spirit. The scarlet figure with the pewter-colored sword and accouterments appeared to grow to gigantic heights, hovering over the ground instead of walking on it.

The scene on the Brocken when the witches gather on May 1 used to make Ellen shiver, reminding her of her childhood when she used to watch the rats scurrying and tumbling over one another in the courtyard of the Princess Theatre.

There were thrilling moments in the duel between Faust and Valentine when Mephistopheles intervened and showers of sparks flew up from the clashing swords to gasps from the audience and to the secret fear of the actors. The swords were linked with very primitive electric mains and the slightest leak in the actors' rubber gloves could give them a most unpleasant shock.

One night, when the Devil seized Faust and they ascended into the flies amid billowing steamy clouds, they missed their footing and fell off the contrivance carrying them skyward. It was only by sheer good luck that they avoided hurtling through the open trap door and down into the cellars beneath. After that, to Ellen's relief, Henry, who was so shortsighted he had to find his way about the stage by guess and instinct, had a pair of spectacles made so small and fine that they were entirely invisible from the front.

What did the public care that it was not a great play when they could be transported from hell to heaven in a single evening? They packed the Lyceum night after night all during

1886, and no new production was needed for the opening of the season in the autumn.

Ellen could not appear in the streets these days without being mobbed by admirers. They queued up outside the stage door just to catch a glimpse of her and Irving leaving the theatre. Young girls dreaming of a stage career besieged her for help. Even when she was visiting her parents, she would be forced to take a hansom cab and slip in and out of the back door to avoid being noticed.

She was trying hard to be both mother and father to the children. Edy was at school in Gloucestershire and doing very well. Soon she was to go to Germany to study music. On coming back from America, Teddy had been sent to a public school, Bradfield College, which he disliked as much as his other schools. Why should he have to learn all these dull subjects, he lamented to his mother, when all he wanted was to be an actor? Ellen was worried about him. From her own childhood she knew the value of hard work. She knew that nothing worthwhile is achieved without a struggle. And everything came to Teddy too easily. If he wanted money, he asked for it and nearly always was given it. He was spoiled and pampered and still very childish for his age. She tried again and again to make him appreciate the advantages which she was able to provide for him.

In later years he remembered being invited to spend several weeks that autumn with Henry at Brook Green, helping him to arrange his library and amusing himself with the dogs, one of which had just had a litter of puppies. Irving, generous as always, gave him books and went out of his way to make his stay a happy one. It was only afterward that Teddy guessed at the reason. It was Ellen of whom Irving was thinking. Edward Godwin had suddenly been taken ill and died on October

6. Whistler, who had remained with him to the end, sent a woman friend to break the news to Ellen. She never forgot the tragic look on Ellen's face and her great cry, "There was no one like him!"

For the rest of her life, Ellen treasured the manuscript of a poem written to his memory,

A man of men, born to be genial King . . .
What others dreamed amiss, he did aright:
His dreams were visions of art's golden age:
Yet self-betrayed, he fell in Fortune's spite,
His royal birthright sold for scanty wage . . .

However unhappy he had made her, he was the one man she had truly loved, the father of her beloved children, and she wept for him as she had not wept for anyone else.

It was a sorrowful year. Fred Archer, the brilliant jockey who had won the Derby only that June and had sent her another fox terrier, Drummie, to join Fussie, had committed suicide in a moment of despair after a serious illness. Although personally he was not so close to her, the loss of a friend from Harpenden days saddened her.

It seemed as if the audiences would never tire of the wonders and visions of *Faust*, and in June of 1887 Irving staged two new productions for a single performance to help break the monotony and boredom of playing the same part night after night.

Werner might have been written by Lord Byron, but it was nothing but gloom, gloom, gloom, thought Ellen, saved only by Henry, who with his marvelous skill contrived to make it interesting. But she had her own fun with *The Amber Heart*. The play had been written for her by Alfred Calmour, secretary to W. G. Wills, a young man she liked and wanted to help. The critics called it romantic fustian, but she loved it. In Ellaline she had one of the gentle, pathetic roles in which she could wring the hearts of her audience with a velvet voice that one of her admirers said was like the heart of a red rose.

Alice Carr designed a dress for her of white muslin, outraging the wardrobe mistress at the Lyceum by boiling it in a potato steamer to get the right "crinkles." It reminded Ellen of Godwin and her Titania dress so long ago at Bristol. Henry put the play on with as much care as if it were to run for a season. In the cast was a young man called Henry Beerbohm Tree whose first contact with Irving both filled him with terror and fired him with a strong ambition to outdo the master one day at his own game of theatre management.

For the first time at the Lyceum, Henry was able to watch Ellen's complete performance from the front. "I wish I could tell you of the dream of beauty you realized," he told her. "Calmour thinks it's all his doing. If he only knew!"

"That's the way of authors," was Ellen's reply. "They imagine so much more about their work than we put into it that to them we are at our best, only doing our duty by them."

For months now, ever since Godwin's death, Henry had been urging her to marry him. He had long wanted to turn their perfect partnership on the stage into a partnership for life. At the back of his mind had always been the hope that Brook Green, where she so often played hostess at his dinner parties, would one day become the home she would share with him as his wife.

But Ellen was wiser than he. She admired him deeply. She loved him and relied on him. He had done more for her than any other man. He had become part of her life, but she knew only too well that his wife would be bitterly revengeful if he were to ask for a divorce. Already she had tried to make scandal about their friendship, poisoning his sons' minds against him. Irving's reaction had been so swift and so icily angry that she had kept a guard over her jealous tongue ever since. But they were public figures. A divorce action would become headline news. In the strict code of Victorian morality it could ruin their careers, hurling them from their lofty position on the stage and in society. And although she knew how much Henry loved and depended on her, she knew too that his art meant more to him than anything else. Without it, he would not be the same person. It was unthinkable that this strange, lonely man who had fought so hard to turn himself into a great actor, who had lifted his profession into a position of such dignity, should, on account of her, lose any part of what he had won.

There were other considerations. Close though she was to him, there were times when she found it difficult to understand this reserved, moody man who so rarely revealed all his inner self even to her. The memory of Kelly and the failure of their marriage was still fresh in her mind.

So she would not say yes, however much he urged her, and he let it rest for the time being while they prepared for their third American tour.

They sailed in November and in all the bustle and turmoil of departure a terrible thing happened. Fussie was left behind on the dock. Charley had died of old age, and to console Henry and because already they had formed a deep attachment, Ellen had given him Fussie.

Both of them were distraught with anxiety during the voyage, and then, to everyone's relief, news reached them in New York that clever little Fussie had justified his long legs and miraculously found his long way home, arriving at his own theatre in the Strand starving and filthy but unharmed.

On this occasion their tour was confined to four cities—New York, Philadelphia, Chicago, and Boston. They opened at the Star Theatre in an appalling blizzard. The cold was so intense that a bunch of violets brought into the dressing room was frozen stiff and brittle as porcelain. Some of the theatres closed down, but the Lyceum Company had never lacked courage or tenacity. They fought their way through a blinding snowstorm and the curtain went up, even if three-quarters of an hour late, to a handful of brave enthusiasts ready to cheer the company's gallantry.

After that freezing start, the weather cleared and *Faust*, produced with all the magical effects and brilliant stage devices brought from England, settled down to a success which swept America off its feet. Two moments on that tour remained in Ellen's memory long afterward. First was a visit to Walt Whitman, the aged poet whose early work had met with so much abuse and whom she and Irving had long admired. In his little house in Philadelphia, Whitman, semi-paralyzed and very frail, sat in his great rocking chair by the hearth and exchanged tales of his stormy youth for gossip about the literary and artistic personalities of London, charmed by Ellen and amused by Henry's dry, sardonic wit.

The second was the unexpected permission to take *The Mer-*

chant of Venice to the strictly guarded Military Academy at West Point. The suggestion had come from Irving and was regarded as so unusual that it had to be submitted to the Secretary of War at Washington. They traveled by special train in the teeth of another raging blizzard, taking only the baskets of costumes and playing on a bare stage as they might have done in Shakespeare's own day. At the fall of the curtain, hundreds of young cadets broke every tradition by throwing up their caps into the air and bursting into thunderous cheers. Irving, leading Ellen forward in her golden dress, remarked dryly that the joybells would be ringing in London that night because for the first time the British had captured West Point.

A week later they sailed for home in time to see the daffodils in the London parks, the clustering pink blossom of the apple orchards, and the sweet, budding hawthorn of an English spring.

Ellen sat on the sea front at Margate and studied the part of Lady Macbeth. It was early November and the holiday travelers had all gone home. She had the English Channel and the long stretches of seaweed-strewn beach to herself.

August had been spent on holiday with Irving and the children at Lucerne in Switzerland. Afterward they had paid a brief visit to Scotland in search of local color. Alas, the "blasted heath" where the Weird Sisters spoke their prophecies to Macbeth and Banquo was now a potato field, singularly flat and uninteresting. "We will have to blast our own heath," she remarked humorously to Irving, amused at his look of disgust.

Lady Macbeth was going to be the greatest test of her skill

as a dramatic actress. "I *must* try to do this: two years ago I could not *even* have tried," she scrawled in the margin of her leather-bound Lyceum copy of the play, beside the great speech that begins "Come, ye spirits that tend on mortal thoughts, unsex me here." The part was a challenge and she was nerving herself to face it. Henry was convinced that she could do it, but then he was in love with her. He thought her perfect every time she set foot on the stage; others would be more critical.

She had not wanted him to put on *Macbeth*. She had longed to play the gay comedy of Rosalind in *As You Like It*, but there was no really suitable part for Henry. It was proving more and more difficult to find plays that had good parts for both of them.

A hundred years ago Mrs. Siddons had played Lady Macbeth as a fiend in human shape, a raging virago, the driving force behind her irresolute husband, a performance which had influenced everyone who had played the part since. But Henry had discovered a book which showed that the great actress had privately held quite a different view. Lady Macbeth is all woman, she had written, loving her husband deeply, exceeding her own strength to win for him what he most desired. It was the only interpretation that made the breakdown in her sleepwalking scene believable, thought Ellen, gazing out over the gray-blue sea, listening to the ceaseless suck of the waves on the shingle beach. Why should she not defy tradition just as Henry had done with Shylock, and create her own Lady Macbeth within the framework Shakespeare had devised?

Alice Comyns Carr had come down to discuss the costumes. She had had a most exciting idea for crocheting the material from twists of heavy green silk shot with blue so that it had the look of both chain mail and the scales of a serpent.

THE NATIONAL PORTRAIT GALLERY

Ellen in MACBETH, *sketch by John Singer Sargent*

"I shall cut it in a flowing medieval design, but how shall we decorate it?" asked Alice.

"With green beetles' wings sewn all over it!" exclaimed Ellen, and laughed at her friend's bewildered face. "Don't you remember?"

Lord Randolph Churchill's beautiful American wife had come to supper at the Beefsteak Room in just such a dress, and they had both been struck by its dramatic possibilities. Lord Randolph had said he had never read Shakepeare until he had seen their Lyceum productions, but from now on he intended to make up for lost time and would make sure that Winston, their fourteen-year-old son, was more attentive to his studies than his father had been.

"The green beetles' wings, with a border of rubies and diamonds in a Celtic pattern," said Alice thoughtfully. "And with it you will wear long red plaits twisted with gold reaching to your knees and a heather-colored cloak embroidered with griffins in flame-colored tinsel."

Made by Mrs. Nettleship, whom Alice had introduced to the Lyceum, the dress looked magnificent, though Oscar Wilde when he saw it at the dress rehearsal remarked wickedly that Lady Macbeth dressed her husband and servants in local homespun but obviously did her own shopping in Byzantium!

Back in London and rehearsing hard, Ellen rocketed between great elation and despair. It was hard to find time to scrawl notes to Edy, who was studying music in Berlin, or to worry about Teddy, who had been at college in Heidelberg and had just been sent home in disgrace after a foolish midnight escapade into the forbidden town.

As always, Henry's work on the crowd scenes was superb. His imagination, always stirred by the weird and the uncanny, created haunting, spine-chilling scenes. Watching him rehearse the last act, when Macbeth at last confronts Macduff, she thought he looked like a great famished wolf, an exhausted giant battling with the merciless power of fate against which no man can prevail. But however busy and exhausted he was, he still found time to give encouragement when despair threatened to overwhelm her.

"Your sensitiveness is so acute that you must suffer sometimes," he wrote to her after a particularly trying rehearsal. "You are not like anybody else. You see things with such lightning quickness and unerring instinct that dull fools like myself grow irritable and impatient sometimes. I feel confused when I'm thinking of one thing and disturbed by another . . . but I do feel sorry afterwards when I don't seem to heed what I so much value . . . You will be splendid in the part. The first time it has been *acted* for many years."

She was in an agony of nerves on the first night, unaware that the critics were leaning forward absorbed, asking themselves: is this Lady Macbeth? It is not in the tradition, but it is new, startling, it is perhaps the interpretation of which Shakespeare dreamed. Not a woman to drive Macbeth forward by physical strength, but more subtly one to madden him into desiring things far beyond his reach. In the sleepwalking scene, her face white with fear, her eyes dark hollows of sleeplessness, she was like a frail, restless spirit haunted by grief and remorse.

Of course opinion was divided, as it always is at a break with the past. And it was her father's praise that pleased her most: "Nellie dear, your performance of Lady Macbeth was *fine*. Don't allow the critics to interfere with your idea of the part . . . It was a grand performance of a most intellectual perception."

Sargent painted her in her beetle-wing dress, an exultant

THE TATE GALLERY

Ellen in her beetle-wing gown as Lady Macbeth, portrait by John Singer Sargent

figure with arms raised high holding the crown triumphantly above her head. When it went on exhibition, dense crowds poured in to gaze at it, and Henry bought it to hang in the Beefsteak Room alongside his Philip II and the portrait of himself painted by Bastien-Lepage which was Ellen's favorite. The artist had exactly caught the quizzical charm, sensitive but intellectual, the rare, elusive smile with which he greeted his guests.

"Wasn't I right?" he said to her one evening when she came into his dressing room as he finished applying his makeup. "You have made the hit of your life, and the public think so too. Now you can begin to enjoy yourself." He smiled into the mirror because they had been arguing about his own performance. Much as she admired his Macbeth, her favorite among his gallery of stage portraits was and always would be Hamlet.

"We'll ask Walter what he thinks," he said mischievously as his dresser helped him into the coat of mail so heavy that he could scarcely lift it from the chair. Henry always insisted that costumes and hand properties should be the real thing and not shams. How else could an actor walk rightly and feel his part?

"Which do you think my best part, Walter?" he asked casually.

The little man hesitated, looking quickly from him to Ellen before he answered: "Why, Macbeth, Mr. Irving. It's got to be."

"Miss Terry prefers Hamlet," remarked Henry.

"Oh no, sir." Walter was very decided. "Oh no, Macbeth. You sweat twice as much in that."

"You see," Henry shrugged and laughed as the call boy knocked on the door and he swung his red cloak around his shoulders and stalked out, every inch the proud, ambitious Scottish chieftain.

Macbeth ran on into the spring, a very busy time for Ellen, who was moving from Longridge Road to Barkston Gardens, only a few streets away but to a much larger house, gay with window boxes, overlooking the trees and green lawns of the square. Here Edy and Teddy could have their own workrooms, though the whole household revolved around Ellen and her work at the Lyceum.

In April they received a royal command to appear before Queen Victoria at Sandringham, the Norfolk home of the Prince of Wales and his wife, Princess Alexandra of Denmark. The Queen had been in retirement since the death of her husband in 1861 and she was more than a little bewildered by the forceful, realistic acting in *The Bells* and the trial scene of *The Merchant of Venice*, so very different from the stately performances of Charles Kean which she remembered from her youth. But she was very gracious when they were presented to her. To Ellen she gave a diamond brooch in the shape of two birds, and the Prince, a delightful host, entertained the players at a festive supper.

It was Teddy who was Ellen's greatest anxiety all that year. What on earth was to be done with him? After being expelled from Heidelberg, he had been sent to study with a tutor in the country but still wrote long, beseeching letters to his mother pleading to be allowed to become an actor. Did he believe an actor's life was all play and no work? Again and again Ellen tried to impress him with little stories about Irving, knowing how much he already admired him.

"You know what happened to me in Boston," she wrote to him once, "when I begged and prayed to be let off one night because of my voice and Henry was like iron—like a rock about it—and I got mad and said, 'I do think that if your son, or your mother, or your wife, the idol of your heart were to die

THE NATIONAL PORTRAIT GALLERY

Henry Irving as painted by Bastien-Lepage. It was Ellen's favorite portrait of Irving

on the stage through making the effort to do the work you would let it happen.' 'Certainly I would,' said he to my utter amazement . . . He would drop himself before he'd give in and there, my Ted, is the simple secret of his great success in everything he undertakes . . . He works so very hard and has worked all his life—that's the meaning of such a brilliant record of successes. Nothing great is done without it, Ted, and oh, believe me, if you were not blind and foolish, you'd understand and will some day and regret how wicked it is of you not to take the golden opportunities you have and profit by them."

It was Henry who came to her rescue, observing her anxiety and the bad effect it was having on her work. He suggested that Ted might be useful to him at the Lyceum.

At seventeen Teddy was an actor with a salary of five pounds a week, far more than he was really worth, but he was Ellen's son. What more could any stage-struck boy want? He would run joyously down the steps of Barkston Gardens each morning and seat himself beside his mother in the one-horse landau. It was like being in a magic boat for two, driving down to rehearsal past Hyde Park Corner, past the grassy stretches of Green Park and into the bustle of broughams, victorias, and hansom cabs crowding around Piccadilly, all jostling and abusing one another. Then along the Strand they went, until they drew up smartly outside the private entrance to the Lyceum, the door that led directly into Henry's office and was used by Ellen but by no other member of the company.

They were rehearsing *The Dead Heart*, a play set at the time of the French Revolution, which was to play that year to coincide with the centenary of the taking of the Bastille. It was a dramatic story of revenge and self-sacrifice. Robert Landry, a sculptor, and the Count de St. Valéry both love Catherine Duval. The Abbé Latour, a scheming and powerful courtier, incites the Count to abduct Catherine and has Landry thrown into the Bastille. Catherine, believing him dead, marries the Count. Eighteen years later comes the Revolution, and Landry, bearded and half blind, staggers out of his cell after years of cruel imprisonment, his one dream to take revenge. He kills the Abbé in a duel, and the young son of his dead rival is hurled into prison and condemned to the guillotine with the other aristocrats. Then by chance Landry meets Catherine and learns for the first time how she was deceived. The old love returns, and to save her beloved Arthur, he takes his place in the tumbril and dies on the scaffold. If the play did not offer Ellen a particularly interesting part, she was amply compensated by seeing Teddy looking so handsome and making such a success as the young Count de St. Valéry.

It was pleasant, too, to act again with old Squire Bancroft, whom Henry had brought out of retirement to play the villainous Abbé. The duel between them was one of the highlights of the production, though it filled Ellen with terror every night. The enthralled audience was quite unaware that the combatants, both accomplished swordsmen, were so shortsighted as to be partially blind without spectacles. Night after night they fought with sabers, laying on so furiously that only the utmost skill kept them from murdering one another.

After the play was done, Teddy would dress quickly and pick up the fine malacca cane with its silver-gilt head that Henry had given him on the first night. He would cross the darkened stage, go up the stairs and into Ellen's dressing room. Some-

ARNOLD ROOD COLLECTION

Ellen and Teddy in THE DEAD HEART

times there would be visitors; sometimes Henry would be there discussing the next day's rehearsal. Then she would finish dressing, put on her hat, pick up her long sealskin wrap, and they would go down together to the waiting carriage and home to supper, set out for them on the sideboard or keeping hot in dishes before the glowing fire.

She would open her pile of letters and smile absently at him while she ate, traces of the evening's performance still clinging about her. Then she would kiss him goodnight and go up to her room.

With all her fame, her popularity, the photographs in the newspapers, the picture postcards, the paragraphs in the gossip columns, Ellen was still a very simple person who loved all the small, everyday pleasures far more than the tinsel gaiety of parties, all the glitter of riotous living that the public associates with the people of the theatre. This was perhaps the greatest link in her friendship with Irving, for he too, beneath the mantle of the great actor-manager, was something of a countryman at heart. His pleasures were few and austere. He loved his books, his pictures, his dogs, and entertaining a few, well-chosen friends to supper and good talk.

These quiet days formed the pattern of Ellen's life and in the year 1890 she was to find a new country home which would give her more delight in the years to come than any of her previous houses.

10
The Twilight of the Gods

WINCHELSEA IS A SMALL, ancient town set high up on a hill overlooking the marshlands stretching down to the sea. Tower Cottage nestles besides the crumbling stone gateway erected by Edward III in the fourteenth century when he rebuilt the town. The gray stone church is a strange shape, broader than it is long because the medieval builders were carried off by the Black Death and when the pestilence had passed there was neither money nor labor to finish it.

Once long ago there had been another Winchelsea on a spur of land thrust out into the swirling waters, until it was destroyed by the hungry sea on a disastrous night of storm and tragedy. Legend said that if you walked close beside the calm waves that had swallowed the stone houses and the thatched barns, you could still hear the elfin ringing of the churchbells and the despairing cries of the villagers trapped in their living tombs.

The light across the marshes was a luminous radiance unlike any to be found anywhere else, and from the high windows of her cottage Ellen could watch the sun set in a bed of flamingo pink and apple green, the gold-etched clouds like fairy castles, just as she had done as a child from the windows of dreary lodging houses all over England.

She had fallen in love with the peace of this gentle countryside. It gave her a freedom that she could never know in London, where all eyes were on her wherever she went. Sometimes in the early morning she would run out into the garden in her thin white nightgown, heedless of neighbors' curious eyes, feeling the grass cool and crisp under her bare feet, breathing deep the honey-sweet smell of the flowers, still as young in heart as the girl who had once lain out all night on the lawn at Harpenden simply to experience the magic of moonlight.

The public who watched their favorite actress chilling as Lady Macbeth, shimmering in wit and laughter as Beatrice, would have gasped to see her on Saturday night throwing a long dust cloak around her shoulders, tying a scarf over the bright hair, and coming out into the night where the pony trap waited. She had always disliked train journeys, so she would take the reins and go cantering down alone through the dark country roads of Surrey and Sussex to reach Winchelsea by dawn.

Pets had a habit of multiplying wherever Ellen lived. Prince, the canary, sang in his gilt cage in the drawing-room window; Minnie, the kitten, watched him out of bright blue eyes before racing after the tortoise, trying to hasten his slow progress over the lawn.

Henry would come down on Sunday to laze in the garden, dozing over the books and playscripts on his lap, Fussie lying at his feet, until Ellen teased him into coming for a drive with her. They would bundle the dogs into the trap and away they would go at a spanking pace down the narrow twisting lanes past orchards of apple, pear, and plum, past the hop-fields and the oast houses, Ellen hanging on for dear life until, laughing, she snatched the reins from him before they all ended up in a turnip field with broken necks.

It was on one of these expeditions that Henry saw a bill in a shop window at Tenterden advertising a performance of Clowe's Marionettes. He insisted on stopping, sought out the proprietor, found out that five pounds was his usual night's takings, and asked if he would put on a show there and then for the same sum. So there they sat, Henry, Ellen, Edy, who was there for the weekend, and Fussie, in the front row of an empty tent and solemnly watched the ingenious one-man performance.

Henry could never resist any type of show, from a circus on the Town Salts at Rye to a humble group of amateurs stumbling through some old melodrama. Performers would whisper excitedly at the sight of the well-known figure in his country tweeds, broad-brimmed hat cocked over one eye, and the lovely golden-haired woman at his side.

Once for a charitable cause Ellen and Edy took part in the village concert, playing two elderly spinsters in a comic sketch that would have made the Lyceum audience open their eyes very wide indeed. The old stone hall with a row of smelly oil lamps for footlights was cold and comfortless, but there was never any question of Ellen putting on the airs and graces of a great actress. She was always just herself, impulsive, warm-hearted, hopelessly scatterbrained, yet shrewd and, with all her apparent carelessness, always able to put her finger on the right thing to say or do.

Even at the Lyceum she would sometimes forget the dignity of her position as leading actress and indulge her sense of fun. That year of 1890 they were preparing *Ravenswood*, an adaptation of Sir Walter Scott's *Bride of Lammermoor*. It was a tragic and gloomy play that Donizetti had turned into a successful opera, but it gave Ellen a good part as the pathetic Lucy Ashton. She looked so enchanting in the riding dress designed for her that every fashionable young woman in London longed to wear a "Ravenswood" coat that season.

The last scene of *Ravenswood* had a remarkable stage effect. The craggy coast and the quicksands where the hero had drowned disappeared in a blackout. The rock-strewn stage cleared and the lights went up to reveal the incoming tide rippling over Kelpie's Flow, a picture of exquisite peace and beauty. It was a wonderful illusion produced by the gradual turning up of concealed lights.

One night Ellen suggested to her young friend, Graham Robertson, that they should hide behind one of the rocks to watch how the effect was produced. The lights faded, the flats began to move, the dead body of Bucklaw played by Terriss was silently drawn off on a sliding plank. As it went by, the corpse gave an audible giggle and whispered, "Look out! Your rock's going next!" With horror they realized he was right. In another moment the dead Bride of Lammermoor would be revealed sitting in the midst of Kelpie's Flow in the white satin and orange blossom of her wedding gown. They had to crawl on hands and knees across the stage, keeping pace behind the moving rock, with Terriss whispering frantic advice from the wings. They got there at last, covered in dust.

"Where's my train?" hissed Ellen.

"Most of it is in my mouth," mumbled Robertson, scrambling after her.

"Thank goodness Henry went straight up to his dressing room," remarked his leading lady with heartfelt relief.

Teddy had the small part of her brother and seemed to have settled into the routine of the Lyceum. Edy had come home from Berlin during the summer, deeply disappointed because severe rheumatism in her hands had brought her career as a pianist to an abrupt end. She was twenty-one and at loose ends, not knowing what she wanted to do with her life. Again Henry came to the rescue with the suggestion that until she had made up her mind she could make herself useful at the Lyceum.

Sometimes Ellen wondered if his own two sons resented the kindness and friendship he extended to her children. Surprisingly, their mother had encouraged their interest in the theatre. Both boys had shown talent in amateur productions, but Henry had sternly disapproved of their taking it up as a career. They had freed themselves from their mother's influence, but though they admired their father and he was generous with gifts and with money, there was no real understanding between them. Harry was at Oxford, reading law and at the same time taking an active part in every student play. Laurence was in St. Petersburg studying Russian and in his spare time was producing plays with himself playing the leading parts, his friends the other roles. With a grim kindness, Henry sent him costumes from the Lyceum wardrobe, even though he disapproved of the venture.

On New Year's Eve Teddy went with Ellen and his sister to dine with Henry at Grafton Street. Only very close friends ever entered this private sanctum. As they climbed the narrow staircase, the ruby-tinted gas lamps lit up the engravings on the walls. They illustrated the history of duelling, one of Irving's passionate interests.

While the others chatted over the wine, Teddy wandered into the adjoining study. Everything there, the pictures of actors of the past on the walls, the books on costume, on history, on every aspect of the theatre crowding on bookshelves and piled up on the floor, spoke of their owner's singlehearted devotion to his art. In a glass case there were the boots worn by Kean in *Richard III*, the sword he had used in *Coriolanus*, the faded green silk purse found empty in his pocket when he died. "How can I more worthily place it than in your hands," wrote Robert Browning when he sent it to Irving after *Macbeth*.

Teddy, still uncertain of what he wanted to do with his life, had a sudden revelation that this would in some way be his own work, to which, like Henry, he would be willing to sacrifice everything. Then he was called in to the other room and the moment vanished.

After dinner they played roulette and other games, shouting with laughter, gambling with newly minted silver coins provided by Henry. Before they left, he brought out his gift for Teddy, an oil painting of David Garrick, with an inscription on the back. Irving, Teddy thought, had the knack of selecting the present you would like most, before you even knew about it.

Nance Oldfield was Ellen's first bid for independence since she had joined Irving. The play, written by Charles Reade, was a gay trifle about the actress who had been the bright star of the Drury Lane Theatre in the early eighteenth century. Anne Oldfield had created the exquisite and witty heroines of Farquhar, Vanbrugh, and Congreve. She enchanted audiences as Mrs. Sullen, Berinthia, and Millament, all ribbons and laces, coming on "full sail, with her fan spread and streamers out, and a shoal of fools for tenders!"

Ellen saw the play, bought it for herself, and with some difficulty persuaded Henry to put it on for her. The part was exactly suited to her. As the actress of whom the poet Richard Savage had written

Beauty, who sways the heart and charms the sight
Whose tongue is music and whose smile delight

she could display her high spirits and sense of fun with a gay wit and tender raillery. It gave Ted a splendid opportunity as the bemused young man whom she teases out of his infatuation for her, all for his own good. It was very well received, even though at the first performance they had both been so uncertain of their lines that they had key speeches written out on slips of paper and strategically placed about the stage.

Henry did not approve of such slipshod behavior. He demanded precision and exactness of technique in every performance. One night in *Ravenswood* she had come off to find him waiting for her in the wings, frowning in annoyance. "Why did you alter your laugh?" he demanded. "It put me out altogether. I was waiting for you to finish."

"I laughed as usual," replied Ellen with indignation.

"No, you didn't. You always say ha-ha seventeen times. You only said it fourteen times tonight."

She stared at him in amazement. She had never worked it out, merely followed her instinct. It was he who had imposed on her an exact rhythm and timing which she had unconsciously followed till that night. "Now I am sure to get it wrong," she thought to herself in despair. "I shall see Henry standing there counting."

It was very rare for Irving to reproach her. Though he could be a tyrant in the theatre and his word was law, with Ellen he was always patient. She sometimes drove him to distraction turning up late for rehearsals or arriving at the theatre only a few moments before she was due on the stage, not because she was deliberately irresponsible but because something had happened that she felt needed her instant attention. Sally Holland would go through agonies waiting for her, terrified in case the Guv'nor should open the communicating door between the two dressing rooms and discover her absence. She would come racing in at the very last moment, her cheeks aglow, humming a gay tune in a way she had if she thought she was to blame for anything.

"That you, Henry?" she said demurely on one such night, sitting down and beginning to make up as he came through the door, watch in hand. "I've been down to the Minories to see someone who sent me a begging letter. I just wanted to make sure that it was genuine."

"The Minories—by the Tower of London!" growled Henry. "A nice place for you at night! I suppose you didn't think of what would happen to the play if you had been attacked by some roughs down there!"

Ellen laughed at him. "Why, every man Jack in the crowd

knew me or had heard tell. I let down the window of the four-wheeler and shook hands with them all. It's because there were so many that I'm so late."

"Of course it's good advertisement," muttered Henry, "but I do wish you wouldn't cut things so fine."

"Not two minutes to your entrance, Miss Terry," yelled Charlie, the call boy, from the passage outside.

"If anybody bothers me I shan't come at all," Ellen replied coolly.

Sally was feverishly slipping garments over her mistress's head and hooking them up while Ellen worked busily with hare's-foot and powder puff.

"Two lines to your speech, Miss Terry, if you please," shrieked Charlie, and Ellen tore down the narrow staircase with Sally running behind holding up the long sweeping skirts to save them from irreparable disaster on some nail or splinter.

"Never know'd such a 'tear-girl,'" she would gasp, coming back to fall exhausted into a chair.

The incident was typical of Ellen's generosity and of her good sense. Appeals for help came with every post, and many a young actress owed her an incalculable debt. She would assist them all through bad patches, but she also gave them good advice. She knew the hardships and disappointments of the theatre too well to encourage stage-struck young girls without talent or training. She would tell them to go away and think it over for a year. To those who possessed something of what she called the "divine power," the qualities of imagination and intelligence she regarded as essential, she would willingly devote both time and money. To one of them, Lynn Fontanne, she gave both a home and encouragement until she found her way to America and her own fame.

Looking back in later years, Ellen thought that *Macbeth* marked the peak of their Lyceum years. They had climbed to the summit of their success and after that, in the words of an unnamed poet Ellen quotes in her diary, "Time that gave did now the gift confound."

They did not perceive it at first. The public still crowded in. They reigned supreme, the sun and moon of the English stage. With so much praise and flattery, it was easy to ignore the warning signs. Expenses had steadily risen, but the takings remained the same. At the Haymarket Theatre, Beerbohm Tree had begun a series of spectacular productions which gradually drew away some of their audiences. For the first time the season showed a loss. They were saved by the profit of a long provincial tour.

Slowly the taste in plays was changing. A Viking wind was blowing out of the North. A Norwegian playwright, Henrik Ibsen, was writing a new kind of drama, bleak and realistic. Many people thought it sordid and unpleasant, but it was startling and it was new.

Henry detested it. He would have agreed with the critic who called *Ghosts* "this morbid and sickening dissection of corrupt humanity." He went one afternoon to see an actress who had been begging his help in *The Doll's House* and came away disgusted. "If that's the kind of thing she wants to play, she'd better play it somewhere else," was his comment.

Ellen was not so sure. She liked the thought of something new, though she could not imagine herself as one of these tortured Scandinavian heroines.

Meantime, it was two years since *Macbeth* and it was good to get back to Shakespeare again, always Ellen's first love. "When I was young and very unhappy," she said to Henry one day, remembering that wretched time after the breakup of her marriage to Watts, "I was very lonely and Shakespeare became my sweetheart. I read everything I could get hold of about my beloved one. I lived with him in his plays." Now she was to play Queen Katharine in Henry VIII in a sumptuous dress designed by Alice in steely silver and bronzy gold with panels of jeweled embroidery. Its only fault was that it was so heavy.

"It's just like a tea tray on my stomach," she lamented one evening in the Beefsteak Room when Sarah Bernhardt was supping with them. "One of my grandmother's, you know, inlaid with mother-of-pearl."

"Ah, but it is just what it should be," said Sarah. "The Tudor touch. So you must not think of your stomach."

Later that same evening, when Henry remarked sadly that old age so fatal to actors must come to all of us, the great French actress leaned toward Ellen, whispering in her broken husky English: "My darling, there are two peoples who shall never be old—you and I."

Bill Terriss had come back to the company, handsome and blustering as the king, but it was Henry who as Cardinal Wolsey in his flame-colored silken robes dominated the play. It was a brilliant study of a man eaten up with pride and ambition. *Henry VIII* is a gorgeous pageant, and Irving, proudly refusing to economize, gave it a magnificent production. But even full houses could not cover the cost.

In the spring, Sarah Terry died suddenly. Ellen mourned her mother, that brave spirit who had cared for her family in so many hard times and had seen so many grandchildren grow up around her. Ben was inconsolable. Ellen, away from the theatre for a few days, came back to find her dressing room filled with daffodils.

"To make it look like sunshine," said Henry.

He had plunged immediately into studying *King Lear*. How like him it was to do such a thing in the full flood of his success as Wolsey. "No conceit, no swelled head—only a fervent endeavor to do better work," she reminded Teddy, who was being a little too casual, a little too carried away by the praise he had received.

She worked on Cordelia down at Winchelsea, finding it difficult—so much to feel, so little to say. "Still waters run deep" seemed the keynote to the character, she thought.

Henry was at Tintagel in Cornwall, climbing up to where the ruins of Arthur's Castle rises jaggedly above the emerald sea. "Where do I find the feather which Lear holds to Cordelia's lips in the last act?" he wrote to her. "Macready used to pluck it out of Edgar's helmet but if I start plucking feathers from Terriss the whole house will roar with laughter." He went on to tell her how he had visited an old woman reputed to be a witch, but Fussie had settled down comfortably on the hearth with the sinister black cat and the only witchcraft he could discover was that the poor old soul somehow lived on four shillings a week. If she knew anything about Henry's generosity, he had done something to remedy that.

Rehearsals started well. All his life Teddy remembered watching his mother, so warm, tender, and loving when Lear wakens from his madness that even in the darkened theatre, with only the amber rehearsal lights, they seemed to be in ancient Britain huddled together in the crumbling ruins of Roman civilization.

Then there was Henry getting up from his chair to show

how the Fool should be played. His voice sounding thin and far off, he feathered on to the stage, floating a couple of steps, alighting on the edge of a table, where he smiled once and then blew out the smile. These were the moments Ellen cherished in her memory forever, the creation of characters he was not down in the program to play, moments of magic when an actor seemed every bit the equal of a poet.

The pity of it was that after so much hard work *King Lear*, produced on November 10, 1892, was a failure. Atmosphere, period, costumes, all were perfect. It was Irving who failed, whose cracked voice of old age could not sustain the tempests of Lear's rages. After all, hadn't Charles Lamb pronounced the part unactable?

"Henry was just marvelous but indistinct from nervousness," she wrote in her diary because she did not want to recall the tragedy of that first night. When the curtain fell to faint applause and audible comments from the audience, he turned to her, bewildered, asking her what had gone wrong, and with the tears running down her face she told him frankly that even she had scarcely been able to understand a word he said.

"Why didn't you tell me before?" he demanded, and she shook her head helplessly, finding it difficult to remind him that in the strain of rehearsal he would not even have heard her.

In a few days he had made a brilliant readjustment, discarding the assumed voice, so that those who came a week later saw a Lear transformed, magnificent and terrible in pathos, but it was too late, the critics had pronounced their verdict.

On the night of November 26, when he returned to his dressing room after the first act, he saw on his table a statuette of himself as Mathias, leaning forward, his face tense, the bag of gold in his hand. On the base was an inscription that told him it was from his comrades of the Lyceum on the twenty-first anniversary of his first performance in *The Bells*. The token of their affection, the certainty that Ellen must have played a large part in it, helped him to overcome the bitter disappointment of his Lear. An actor has to learn to take failure in his stride if he is not to be defeated by it.

One unexpected pleasure was in store for him. Laurence had returned from Russia and, still determined to take up the life of an actor, had obtained a part in *Walker, London,* a comedy by a new young Scottish playwright, J. M. Barrie. He came to the Lyceum that winter and a new and warmer feeling grew up between him and his father. When he came of age in December, Irving bought two magnificent gold watches, one for him and one for Ted, who would be twenty-one in January.

It was at this time that Ellen met Laurence for the first time, and almost against his will, he fell under her spell. He had always seen her through his mother's prejudiced eyes as the evil influence in his father's life. Now suddenly he realized her beauty, her charm, the generosity of her friendship. She liked him instantly. "My Irving boy," she called him. She listened sympathetically when he confided to her that he was writing a play. She promised to do all she could to persuade his father to take an interest in it. Next year they would be going again to America. There, with no new productions to occupy them, there would be leisure to read and consider it.

"When the dumb Hour, clothed in black,
Brings the Dreams about my bed,
Call me not so often back,
Silent Voices of the dead,
Toward the lowland ways behind me,
And the sunlight that is gone!"

sang the choir as Tennyson's coffin, wrapped in its flag, was carried up the aisle of Westminster Abbey. Ellen felt the poet's beautiful lines, set to music by his wife, were a better memorial to him than the spoken tribute.

The poet had died just a month before the opening of *King Lear.* She looked around at the congregation and thought no face there looked anything alongside Henry's. The hair that had been raven black was now touched with silver. He was very pale and slim and wonderful. "The head of a saint," Sargent had exclaimed the day Henry had come to the studio when he was painting her as Lady Macbeth. And it seemed as if he would be playing a saint during the coming year. He had long been working on an acting version of Tennyson's play on Thomas à Becket, the great Archbishop who was murdered in Canterbury Cathedral by Henry II's turbulent knights.

Ellen sighed because, although she admired the play, there was so little chance in it for her. The part of Rosamund de Clifford, the king's mistress, whom Becket protects against the vengeance of Queen Eleanor, was no more than a charming trifle brought in quite unhistorically to lighten the tragedy.

After the failure of Lear, rehearsals for *Becket* began early in the New Year. One morning Terriss came in very late and soaked to the skin.

"Is it raining, Bill?" asked someone teasingly, surprised to see him so wet.

"Looks like it, doesn't it?" was the casual reply.

"We've been waiting for you," snapped Henry. "Get yourself into something dry and be quick about it."

In no time, Terriss was back. Grimly, Henry took him through his scenes with Ellen. He was playing the Plantagenet king, Henry II, with all his usual vigor and charm. More than fifty times he vaulted across the table to make a spectacular exit before Irving pronounced himself satisfied and dismissed him. He strolled off with a nod and wink at Ellen. It was only by chance that they discovered afterward that he had dived into the Thames that morning and saved a child from drowning.

Becket had its first night on February 6, Henry's fifty-fifth birthday. Ellen had performed a miracle with her small part, unrewarding though it was, giving it grace and tenderness. She looked her loveliest in a Renaissance gown of pale gold and glowing color, her bright hair caught in a golden net. Her heart-rending cry when she ran on after the murder drew together all the anguish, pity, and horror at the sacrilege. She did not envy Henry his personal triumph. She was only glad that the bitterness of Lear should be wiped away by the unstinted praise he received for the strength and nobility of his portrayal of the martyred saint.

Teddy, as the youngest Lord Templar, contrived to fluff his few lines but was fortunate enough to escape notice. He enjoyed himself thoroughly at the first-night party when the distinguished visitors surged up on to the stage for a buffet supper. As Ellen's son he was one of the privileged few from the company who were present on these occasions.

Invitations to Beefsteak suppers were eagerly sought after. That year Princess Mary of Teck, who was to marry Prince George and become Queen Mary of England, was entertained with her parents. Frequent visitors were Burne-Jones, Arthur Sullivan, who was writing the music for Gilbert's witty operettas at the Savoy, and Oscar Wilde, whose *Lady Windermere's Fan* had caused a sensation at the St. James's Theatre. Ironically, not one of those who enjoyed the Lyceum's lavish hospitality had the slightest inkling of the anxieties which had begun to cloud the horizon.

Henry was a marvelous host. Watching the pale, ascetic face against the dark paneling, Ellen thought of what Keats had written in one of his letters, that the poet lives not in one but in a thousand worlds. Surely that was true of an actor of great imagination. There were so many Irvings—the dedicated actor, the stern idealist of the theatre, the sensitive boy who never quite forgot his pious upbringing, the sardonic, amusing companion whose witty conversation could be sharp but was rarely unkind. Sometimes he indulged a mischievous sense of humor at the expense of his devoted staff, who obeyed his slightest whim without question.

One day when she was talking to him in his dressing room, he had idly taken a white lily from a bowl on his table and began to dot and stripe the petals with the stick of greasepaint. He held it out to her. "Pretty, isn't it?"

"Oh, don't be ridiculous, Henry," she said, laughing.

"You wait," he grinned. "We'll show it to Loveday."

When his stage manager came in, solemn as usual, with some query about the evening performance, Henry again held out the flower. "Pretty, don't you think?"

"Very," said Loveday. "I always like those lilies. A friend

of mine has a garden full of 'em and he says they're not difficult to grow if you give 'em enough water."

Henry's eyes sparkled with childish amusement at the success of his little joke, but Ellen wondered whether Loveday saw through it but in his affection would not spoil the Guv'nor's bit of fun.

In March the Queen commanded them to present *Becket* at Windsor Castle on the occasion of a visit from her daughter, the Empress Frederick of Germany. The scenes were all produced in miniature in the Waterloo Chamber, and the Empress wrote in her diary: "Ellen Terry as Rosamund was perfect, so graceful and full of feeling and so young-looking in her lovely light dress . . . She is very tall, pleasing and ladylike."

As was usual in those days, the theatre closed for Holy Week, and Ellen, down at Winchelsea, received an unexpected telegram from Teddy announcing his marriage to May Gibson, daughter of old Harpenden friends, whom he had known since childhood. It came as a shock. Ellen had been aware of their attachment but had not considered it serious. Only a few weeks before, she had written to him about their coming American tour, pointing out that he would come home with three hundred pounds in his pocket. Now it would be out of the question. Henry would certainly not permit him to bring a young wife with him. She thought him far too young to know his own mind, far too irresponsible for marriage, and she was right. But Teddy had suddenly rebelled. He was of age, he was determined to go his own way, forgetting that he had little money except what his mother had saved for him out of his salary, that he had no work except what Irving was kind enough to give him. He and May would be dependent on Ellen's generosity.

She sighed over him, but there was nothing she could do. She owned a tiny seventeenth-century cottage at Uxbridge by the side of a river where ducks nested in the reeds of the wooded banks. She would have liked to give it to him but felt that it would not be for his good. It was high time he learned to stand on his own feet. She let it to the young couple at the nominal rent of five shillings a week and began to prepare for the fourth American tour.

Except that this time they opened in the Grand Opera House in San Francisco and played a number of towns in the West, where they had not been seen before, the tour followed the same pattern as before. Fussie, as usual, gave them an anxious moment. As they drew out of New York, they discovered that the dog had disappeared. Henry commanded the train to be held up, a search was made, and then a little white figure came into view marching resolutely down the railway track. Fussie was on his way to California.

The most delightful memory for Ellen was the success of *Nance Oldfield*. It was played in a double bill with *The Bells* and was received with rapture wherever they went. Though she missed Teddy in it, she had to be content with the young Martin Harvey playing the boy lover.

"It proves how much I love you that I'm not jealous," said Henry, smiling as she came off after innumerable curtain calls. She had always been level-headed and modest about her own successes. She deeply admired Henry and was utterly loyal to him, but now and again she found herself wishing that he would use her more in the type of part in which she excelled. She had been given so few opportunities to play comedy lately. A tiny spark of discontent was burning in her heart, and when they returned to England there was someone waiting who would do his utmost to blow it into flame.

Before they left for America, Joe and Alice Comyns Carr had invited Ellen and Irving to dine with them one evening so that afterward Joe could read his play on the theme of King Arthur. Henry was not an encouraging audience. He lay back in his deep armchair, his eyes closed, and did not utter a word. The author struggled on and had just reached his most moving passages when he was interrupted by loud and prolonged snores.

"I don't believe it's any use for me to go on, Henry," said Joe, hurt and disappointed. "It seems to be boring you."

"Don't be silly. He's not the one that's snoring!" laughed Ellen, and pointed to Fussie, curled up on his master's lap fast asleep.

Fortunately, neither Ellen nor Irving were of Fussie's opinion. They liked the play. They took it to America with them and studied it while they were away. The great success of the tour had brought fresh funds into the depleted coffers of the Lyceum. Henry, who was always optimistic, forgot his anxieties and was prepared to throw everything into the most splendid production ever presented at the theatre. Burne-Jones was asked to design the settings, Arthur Sullivan would compose the music, Johnston Forbes-Robertson came back to play Lancelot with Henry as Arthur and Ellen as Guinevere.

Alice designed dresses for Ellen that were dreams of beauty, except that the weight nearly killed her. She said so in no uncertain terms when she swept on at the dress rehearsal in a silver cloak embroidered all over with gold and turquoises.

"Oh, do keep it as it is," cried Alice from her place in the stalls. "It looks splendid."

"I can't breathe in it, much less act," exclaimed Ellen. "For heaven's sake send someone to cut off a few stones!"

Reluctantly Mrs. Nettleship with her assistants came up to snip off a jewel here and there. By the time they had finished, they had gathered a basketful which their united efforts could not lift from the floor!

Burne-Jones, tall and frail, with thin gray hair and blue eyes very bright and clear under a massive forehead, stared in amazement and dismay at the transformation of his exquisite Pre-Raphaelite designs into the dramatic stage pictures painted by Hawes Craven. When she was not on the stage, Ellen would sit with him in the stage box. They would whisper together, eating chocolate to stave off hunger and falling into helpless giggles when a giant May tree came on and Henry's voice rose in agony from the stalls. "Take away that confounded tree! It looks like a great cauliflower."

Then there was Sullivan, accustomed to opera rehearsals where the music was all important, tapping impatiently with his baton during an interminable pause while scenery was being laboriously changed.

"What are we waiting for?" he demanded imperiously. "Irving, are you ready?"

The curtains parted. Henry, magnificent in black Gothic armor, eyeglasses perched perilously on his thin nose, stalked slowly down to the footlights. "Ready?" he snapped. "Ready for what?"

"Shame, I calls it," commented the charlady, broom in hand, pausing in her work just behind Ellen. " 'E don't care for no one. It's just the same with me. Look 'ow 'e messes up my stage just when I've cleaned it!"

The frayed nerves and lost tempers of dress rehearsals are all forgotten in the success of a first night. When the curtain went up on January 12, 1895, the audience gasped at Arthur's Hall in Camelot hung with rich tapestries, with the three great arches at the back through which a river could be seen winding down to a silver sea.

The production seemed to sum up all the arts and sentiments of Victorian England just when the forces were gathering that would sweep away the romantic idealism of the past and make room for new ideas, harsher, more realistic, more matter-of-fact.

Praise was poured out from every quarter but one. The new drama critic on the *Saturday Review* expressed quite different opinions. "I sometimes wonder where Mr. Irving will go to when he dies—whether he will dare to claim as a master artist to walk where he may one day meet Shakespeare whom he has mutilated, Goethe whom he has travestied and the nameless creator of the hero-king out of whose mouth he has uttered jobbing verses," he wrote acidly.

Well, that was bad enough, but Henry could afford to laugh, with the public fighting for seats. What followed struck at him more closely, penetrating the armor of his reserve. "As to Miss Ellen Terry, it was the old story, a born actress of real women's parts condemned to figure as a mere artist's model in costume plays which, from the women's point of view, are foolish flatteries written by gentlemen for gentlemen . . . a heartless waste of an exquisite talent. What a theatre for a woman of genius to be attached to!"

The article was signed with the initials G.B.S.

The red-haired, red-bearded Irishman, George Bernard Shaw,

was at this time in his late thirties. He had left Dublin in 1876 determined to make his fortune in London. He had starved while he wrote three novels that turned into dismal failures. He tried his hand at journalism and in 1884, almost in despair, became music critic on *The World*. Now promoted to the *Saturday Review*, he became an eager member of the audience at the Lyceum. With three unsuccessful plays behind him, he was fighting for recognition as a playwright. He had just put the finishing touches to a new one-act play, *Man of Destiny*, a comedy about Napoleon and a Strange Lady, which he declared he had written entirely for Ellen.

With her help Shaw had high hopes of persuading Irving to put it on for him, but he could not resist attacking him for his adherence to a type of drama he considered old-fashioned and out-of-date. To Ellen—approaching middle age, a grandmother now, since Ted and May had a baby daughter, and a little disappointed with the parts she had been playing—the audacious letters which this provocative, brilliant Irishman had begun to write her, sometimes daily, were a stimulation and a challenge. Soon he was proclaiming himself in love with her, the exquisite actress he had seen and admired when he first came to London and had never yet met.

He both amused and fascinated her. He sent her his book *The Quintessence of Ibsenism*. He had the impudence to tell her how to act in Shakespeare, she who had made him her familiar companion since the age of five, she of whom people said that she spoke the language of Shakespeare as if it were her native tongue! The audacity of the man! He dubbed Irving the Ogre who had shut her up in the dark castle of the Lyceum and kept her there imprisoned until he, like Childe Roland in the legend, should come to her rescue.

It was absurd, but it was clever. It was a mocking but unusual overturning of all conventional ideas. In the circles in which Ellen moved, he was regarded with contempt, an uncouth Irishman with no manners, sniping at everything which they valued. Henry could not understand her interest in him, but Ellen recognized the genius behind the boasting, the vanity, the destructive criticism. She defended Irving vigorously against his attacks, laughed at his jests, and thoroughly enjoyed herself writing brilliant and witty letters in reply.

Shaw, however, did not represent the view of the majority of the English toward Irving. On May 24 Irving appeared on the doorstep of Ellen's home with the news that he had been offered a knighthood. For the first time in the history of the stage an actor, still a rogue and vagabond on the statute books, was to receive the honor of the Queen's accolade. In July he was summoned to Windsor Castle to receive his new dignity at the hands of Queen Victoria. The next day the actors and actresses of London and as many as could make the journey from the provinces gathered at the Lyceum to present him with a congratulatory address. With iron determination he had progressed from a lanky, stammering, awkward boy to the head of his profession. "In olden times," he said to them, "our Britons showed their appreciation of a comrade by lifting him on their shoulders and I cannot but feel it with an unspeakable pride that you, my brothers in our art, have lifted me on your shields. There is no more honor to come into the life of a man so raised."

Ellen wrote in her diary: "The dear fellow deserves any honor, all honors. He is just as pleased about it as he should be and I'm much pleased too."

They had not anticipated it when they planned their fifth

American tour. It shed an added glamour around them wherever they went. When they sailed for New York at the end of September, Laurence came to see them off at Liverpool, his hopes high, for in her baggage Ellen carried his play and she had promised to persuade his father to put it on, herself to play the leading part.

11
The End of the Lyceum

THE RETURN HOME from the United States was a sad one. Floss, Ellen's beloved younger sister, who had married and left the stage, died while she was away, and when the ship docked, she was greeted with the news that her father had caught one of his winter colds and succumbed to the ensuing pneumonia. It was heartbreaking to know that Ben was gone, but the Terry genius lived on in the family he had founded: in Ellen, Marion, and Fred, and in the grandchildren, who were already beginning to show their precocious talents.

Still it was good to be able to tell Laurence that they had

produced his *Yolande and Godefroi* in Chicago and it had been well received despite its grim theme. No one before had ever dared to write a play whose heroine is stricken with leprosy. The Victorians preferred to forget the unpleasant side of life. Henry would have thrown it aside but for Ellen's urging.

"We have fourteen plays in the repertory already," he said. "Surely that's enough. It's not a part for you."

But Ellen was determined. She had given her promise and would not go back on it. She persuaded the company to play in it, she enlisted the help of the stagehands. Edy, who had traveled with them, devised scenery and costumes out of existing stocks.

Ellen liked the spare modern writing. She enjoyed the gasp of the audience when she made her entrance in a scarlet gown, her face blanched paper-white, crimson flowers in her gold hair, playing the beautiful, despairing Yolande, deserted in her sickness by her princely admirers and saved by the humble steward whose love she has spurned.

Henry was forced to change his mind. They played it in other cities with equal success. When the usual mob of journalists swarmed around him as he came off the ship at Liverpool, she heard the pride in his voice when he spoke of his clever son. The joy on Laurence's face at the praise was reward enough.

Harry too was on better terms with his father. He had become engaged to a young actress who had won all hearts as Trilby in the play adapted from George du Maurier's famous novel. Ellen sent the young couple a grandfather clock as a wedding present and went down to Winchelsea for a few weeks' holiday before studying her new part.

It was like going back to the golden days to be rehearsing *Cymbeline* that August. Ellen had long wanted to play Imogen. Swinburne, the poet, called her the "flower crown" of Shakespeare's heroines. Dignity under a false accusation, unwavering love in spite of persecution, must have had a special appeal for Shakespeare, she noted in her copy of the play, for he exalted these traits in Imogen as he had done in Queen Katharine and in Hermione in *The Winter's Tale*. Bernard Shaw was writing her long letters instructing her how she should play the part. She did not take them very seriously.

Ted remembered that when he had to carry her into the cave at her supposed death, she seemed light as a feather in his arms though ordinarily he could not have lifted her easily. The miracle of Ellen Terry, he thought. She *was* Imogen, or Imogen was she—he did not know which.

The production of this little-known play justified Henry's experiment. The fine settings had been designed by the Dutch artist Alma-Tadema. As for Ellen, she was "such a radiant embodiment of youth that when she first appeared the audience gasped . . . she seemed a creature of fire and air, she hovered over the stage without appearing to touch it," wrote Graham Robertson, "and as a companion picture was Irving's Iachimo, no scowling sinister villain, but a fascinating Italian gentleman, entirely without morals, but with exquisite manners and compelling charm."

For some time Ellen had been having difficulty with her eyes, and after a successful ten weeks, she followed her doctor's advice and went to Germany for a course of special treatment, while Henry prepared *Richard III*, a play in which the women's parts were not of sufficient importance to require her presence.

The success of the first night was so tremendous that it seemed to Ellen when the news reached her that the great days of the Lyceum had surely returned. But it was at this very moment that misfortune hit them. Returning home exhausted from the strain of the performance and from playing host to more than five hundred guests, Irving tripped and fell heavily on the narrow stairs of his lodgings. He managed to crawl to his bedroom, but the next day he was unable to move. He had torn the ligaments in his knee. For the first time in his life he who had never been ill for more than a few days was forced to rest for several weeks. The theatre had to close.

Bernard Shaw, resentful and angry at the rejection of his *Man of Destiny*, lashed out in biting criticism of Irving's portrayal of Richard III and received a stinging reply from Ellen. "If you worry (or try to worry) Henry I must end our long and close friendship. He is ill and what would I not do to better him." She hurried back from Germany, but not even her presence could save the theatre. Without Irving's magnetic personality, the audience fell away.

At Grafton Street she sat by his sofa and, to help him pass the time, read two acts of Ibsen's *John Gabriel Borkman* to him. He was not impressed.

As soon as he was on his feet again, they began to rehearse Sardou's *Madame Sans-Gêne*. The title role was that of a spirited washerwoman who has risen to become Duchess of Danzig in Napoleon's court but still retains her old rough-and-ready peasant manners. In the great scene of the play, the Emperor commands her to divorce her husband and leave Paris. She vigorously reminds him they were comrades in the days of the Revolution and triumphantly waves under his nose a laundry bill he had neglected to pay.

Réjane, the great French actress, had played the part in London and Paris. Irving put it on solely for Ellen, and she rose to the challenge magnificently, reveling in a chance to play good, rollicking comedy. Henry found it more difficult to button himself into the short stocky Napoleon. He was too tall, lean, and austere.

In the royal box on the first night the Prince of Wales patted him on the shoulder. "Sir Henry, you should not play Napoleon. Wellington perhaps, not Napoleon." But his uncle, the old Duke of Cambridge, who had danced with Ellen when she was a child, was thumping her on the back enthusiastically. "Ah, m'dear," he grunted, "*you* can act!"

Unfortunately, in this year of 1897 they were having to compete with Diamond Jubilee celebrations. Victoria had reigned for sixty years and every Englishman worthy of the name was eager to pay homage to the stout little lady in her black dress and white bonnet, waving from her carriage with the six matched gray horses.

It seemed as if nothing could go right. While they were on tour in Manchester in December, a carpenter carelessly threw his coat on stage with a ham sandwich in the pocket. Fussie, who loved food far too well, went nosing after it, fell through the open trap door, and was killed instantly. Horrified, the cast ran to tell Ellen. No one dared to break the news to Henry until after the evening performance. He took it quietly, saying little, and next day carried the little body back to London wrapped in a rug. Fussie was given an honorable burial in the dogs' cemetery in Hyde Park.

Back at the Lyceum, Ellen worried, knowing how grievously Henry would miss the little terrier in his dressing room after so many years. Then a strange thing happened. The theatre cat, who had never before shown the slightest interest in anybody, came in and sat on Fussie's cushion. They held their breath. No one knew how the Guv'nor would take it. When Walter was sent out to buy some meat, Ellen breathed a sigh of relief. From then on, the cat always sat night after night in the same place and Henry seemed to like its silent companionship. Years later, when he left the Lyceum forever, he wrote to tell her that he had taken the cat with him.

Troubles never come singly, they say, and certainly it seemed so in the months that followed. Five days after Fussie had gone, William Terriss was stabbed to death outside the stage door of the Adelphi Theatre by a half-crazy, small-part actor with an imaginary grievance. The shock was terrible. Ellen sorrowed for the gay, good-natured man who had been one of her oldest friends. His death seemed all the more cruel in that he had just written to Henry asking if he might return to the Lyceum after his present engagement. Irving went at once to visit his widow and did everything he could to assist his dependents.

They had scarcely recovered from the loss of their comrade when a fresh calamity struck. The scenery store where the settings for forty-four plays were stacked, acres of canvas designed by some of the greatest artists of the day, caught fire and burned to ashes. All the scene painters in England working for a year, it was said, could not replace what disappeared in a single night's holocaust, and the insurance did not cover a quarter of the value.

Together, they weathered the shock. Ellen, whose loyalty would never have permitted her to desert a friend in need, had no thought of breaking their partnership, though the new productions gave her little opportunity. Henry had been persuaded to put on Laurence's new play, *Peter the Great*. It was an interesting study of the relationship between the great

Russian tsar and his unhappy son. In it Ellen played the small part of Peter's second wife, Catherine. It could not keep the Lyceum open. They were forced to set out on long provincial tours, suffering all the hardships of drafty theatres and uncomfortable hotels during the worst of winter.

In Glasgow Henry caught a severe cold. With a high temperature he struggled through *Madame Sans-Gêne*. The next day, pneumonia set in, and this time he was gravely ill. The tour from which they had hoped so much dwindled to nothing without him.

"When I think of Henry's work during these years I could weep," wrote Ellen in her diary at this time. "Never was there a more admirable extraordinary worker; never had anyone more courage and patience. Blow after blow . . . yet he never complained, never spoke bitterly of bad luck. One night when his cough was rending him and he could hardly stand for weakness, he acted so brilliantly and powerfully that it was easy to believe in the triumph of mind over matter."

He made a slow and painful recovery, only to discover that too much had been lost. He did not have sufficient funds to continue as sole manager of the Lyceum. It had to be turned into a company, which would give him only limited control.

Once Ellen had said with a merry twinkle in her eye, "Were I to be run over by a steam roller tomorrow, Henry would be deeply grieved; would say quietly, 'What a pity!' and would add after two minutes' reflection, 'Who is there . . . er . . . to go on for her tonight?' " Now it seemed as if her jest had come true. His plans did not take her into consideration at all. It was difficult for her to realize that Irving, with almost everything he valued—health, strength, control over his company—slipping away from him, was able to hold on to one thing only. He had to go on acting. There was nothing else left in life that meant anything to him.

For three more years Ellen acted with him whenever she was wanted. She went to America playing a tiny part in *Robespierre*, the new play Sardou had written for him. It was the last production to carry something of the glitter and glory of the Lyceum. Henry, forced to economize, asked Edy to design and make the costumes and she did it brilliantly, creating richness and dramatic effect out of yards of cheap sateen, flannelette, and bargains from a coster's barrow. Her success gave her the impetus to start up for herself as a designer of theatrical costumes. But the play provided little of interest for Ellen.

There was one more Shakespearean production, *Coriolanus*, with splendid settings by Alma-Tadema and with all Henry's magic in the crowd scenes, but they rehearsed in a London shrouded in gloom, the streets hung with crepe at the death of the old Queen. It was an unlucky play and Ellen never felt happy as the Roman matron Volumnia.

Times had changed. Now at the turn of the century they were having to face vigorous opposition. Where once there had been only three theatres presenting serious drama, now there were fourteen. The intellectual playgoing public they had helped to create was turning to new and different types of entertainment.

Ellen's brilliant success of these years was in a production Henry released her to play in—*The Merry Wives of Windsor*, with Beerbohm Tree, at His Majesty's, Tree's splendid new theatre in the Haymarket. "Heaven give you many many merry days and nights," Henry said to her in his first-night telegram. How she reveled in the gay comedy of Mistress Page! She had always loved to make people laugh, and how they roared at the merry tricks the two wives played on the stout Falstaff! How they stormed the stage door with flowers and gifts and even love letters! At her age! She laughed at the very idea, but how enjoyable it all was.

She was still playing matinees at the Lyceum. This was Coronation Year, and London had thrown off its trappings of woe and was decked with flags and bunting. The Prince of Wales had become Edward VII. In July, Irving in a last extravagant gesture held the most magnificent of all his theatrical parties. The Lyceum was transformed into an exotic jungle of palms, flowers, and shrubs, the stage hung with scarlet velvet and painted satin, the floor covered with crimson carpet. It was an Arabian Night's entertainment. The guests, gathered in London for the Coronation, came from all over the Empire: Indian princes in robes stiff with jewels, maharajahs and sultans, foreign ambassadors and princes with their wives glittering in diamonds, their ostrich-feather fans rivaling the brilliant tribal dress of the Africans. And at the center stood Henry with his two sons and Ellen beside him, her radiance undimmed, seeming as always to make every other woman look insignificant.

The season ended on July 19 with *The Merchant of Venice*. As Henry led Ellen forward, they both knew that the Lyceum was doomed, though the applause rocked the old building to the very roof. When the curtain fell for the last time, they turned to each other. Ellen's eyes were filled with tears. "I shall never be in this theatre again," she whispered, trembling. "I feel it, I know it."

That autumn Henry was to set out on a provincial tour without her. His new play, *Dante*, had no part for her. He had commissioned it from Sardou and with reckless courage presented it at the Drury Lane Theatre with a huge cast in a lavish production. When he took it to America in 1903, Ellen refused his generous offer. She would not accept a high salary for which she would be required to do so little. There was no bitterness, no harsh words at their parting. The partnership of nearly twenty-five years had come to an end, but the deep affection was there still.

In the early months of 1905 news came to Ellen in London that Henry had been taken seriously ill in Wolverhampton and his tour had been abandoned. It was two years since they had acted together, but the ties of friendship had never been broken. She dropped everything and left for the Midlands.

As the train jogged along through fields bleak and wintry under a thin February sun, she thought back over the last years. Her first venture into management had not been successful. She had lost a great deal of money putting on Ibsen's *The Vikings* simply to please Teddy. He had produced it wonderfully; his settings, new, imaginative, and exciting, had won high praise. It seemed to her that the genius of Edward Godwin was beginning to flower in her son, and generously she had wanted to help him as much as she could, and Edy too, whose workroom had not yet shown any profit. But she had never felt pleased with herself as the savage and barbaric Hjordis.

She had gone to Stratford-on-Avon one April to play Queen Katharine in *Henry VIII* at the Birthday Festival. She was fulfilling a promise she had made to the boy who had once tried to teach them all how to play *Romeo and Juliet*. Frank Benson's Shakespearean Company had become known all over England. She felt proud when he told her that his one aim had been to create his company in the spirit of the Lyceum.

Next year, in 1906, she would be on the stage for fifty years —fifty years since she had played Mamillius, tripped over her toy cart, and thought her career finished forever.

The train was late at Wolverhampton and she went to a hotel for the night. The next morning, her arms filled with daffodils, she was on her way to visit Henry. "It is his heart," his doctor had told her. "Whatever happens, he must never play Mathias in *The Bells* again."

"Fiddle!" said Henry when gently she tried to impress on him that he must take care. He had always refused to admit any bodily weakness. "It's not my heart at all. It was that rug at the door. I tripped over it."

Sitting up in bed with his old dressing gown draped around his shoulders, he looked, she thought, like some beautiful gray tree she had seen years ago in Savannah. "I'm glad you've come," he said with the smile that always charmed her. "Two queens have been kind to me this morning. Queen Alexandra telegraphed . . . and now you . . ."

They spoke a little of their work, as actors always do, and then Ellen, seeing his whole splendid career in one flash of memory, exclaimed, "What a wonderful life you've had, haven't you?"

"Oh yes," he answered quietly. "A wonderful life—of work."

"And there's nothing better after all, is there?"

"Nothing."

"Do you ever think, as I do sometimes, what you have got out of it all?"

"What have I got out of it?" He smiled. "Let me see . . .

a good cigar, a good glass of wine, good friends." And he picked up her hand, kissing it gently.

"Not a bad summing up," she said. "And the end . . . how would you like that to come?"

"How would I like that to come?" He was silent for a few moments. Then he snapped his fingers. "Like that."

Eight months later Ellen was to remember his words. She was playing in *Alice-sit-by-the-fire,* which J. M. Barrie, the Scottish playwright, had written especially for her. On October 14 her maid burst into her bedroom early one morning. "Mistress dear," she began, and her voice choked. "Mistress dear, there is dreadful news. Sir Henry . . ."

Ellen stopped her with a gesture. "I know . . . leave me quite alone."

He had died as he had wished. He had played Becket as well as he had ever played it, come quietly out of the stage door, signed his autograph for a boy who was patiently waiting, said a kind word to his stage manager, who had not been well, and stepped into the waiting cab. In the doorway of his hotel, he slipped to the floor and was gone.

An actor never breaks faith with his audience. Loyal to the tradition in which she had grown up, Ellen went to the theatre that night, but when she reached the line, "It's summer done, autumn begun . . . I had a beautiful husband once, black as raven was his hair . . ." she could not go on. The sobs caught in her throat. The curtain was lowered and the audience went quietly home.

The flags were flying at half mast, the pillars of the Lyceum were hung with crepe, and every London cab driver had tied a black bow on his whip the day they brought Irving to Westminster Abbey.

A magnificent tawny sun sent shafts of golden light across the old gray stone at the very moment the coffin under its pall of laurel leaves was carried up the choir. "How Henry would have loved it!" Ellen thought. Almost she could see him beside her directing the whole impressive ceremony, saying impatiently, "Get on! Get on!" when the service dragged.

They laid him beneath the statue of Shakespeare they had both loved, and beside his fellow actor David Garrick.

As she came out of the great doors, her tear-filled eyes dazzled by the sunshine, she felt lost for a moment. It was like those times at the Lyceum when he had disappeared into his office for a while and the rehearsal was all at odds until he came back.

She must hurry. There was the train back to Manchester for the evening performance. Whatever happened, she must not miss it. That was something Henry would never have forgiven.

"What did you feel in there, Miss Terry?" asked a reporter, thrusting impudently close to her.

"He was a great actor, a great friend, and a good man," she answered as she moved quickly away. "What more is there to say?"

Epilogue

SMALLHYTHE PLACE IS a small Tudor farmhouse on the edge of the marsh. Four centuries ago a long arm of the sea had lapped at its very doors. The harbor master had lived there and ships had been built on the strand. But now the waters had receded. There was only the narrow stream babbling along beside the garden with reeds and grasses whispering at its brink, the cry of the curlews and plovers overhead, the whir of bats' wings in the early dusk, and sometimes on warm moonlit nights the song of the nightingale in the woods opposite.

Ellen and Henry had found it together on one of their excursions from Winchelsea. A few miles from Tenterden, it lay wrapped in the peace of the quiet Kentish countryside. Henry VIII, so legend said, had come wooing Anne Boleyn

ELLEN TERRY MEMORIAL

Ellen's home at Smallhythe, now the Ellen Terry Memorial

ELLEN TERRY MEMORIAL

Ellen's bedroom at Smallhythe. The desks by the window are those used by Edy and Teddy when they were children

there when she lived in nearby Yew Cottage. Ellen had loved it at once, only it had not been up for sale. But she had never forgotten. As soon as it came into the market, she bought it. This was the house, she felt, where she would like to grow old.

Early in June of 1906 she was out in the garden, an old straw hat like a big mushroom tied on over the still-bright hair. Armed with leather gloves and a pair of scissors, she was snipping away at the roses that climbed up the porch. Madonna lilies, snapdragons, sweet williams, columbines, and old-fashioned clove pinks jostled one another along the flagged paths and filled the air with the sweet dry scents of summer.

Edy came hurrying from the house with a sheaf of telegrams in her hands. They sat down on the wooden bench to tear them open, exclaiming in delight and wonder while the dogs came racing up to find out what all the excitement was about.

When the suggestion had been made that there should be a celebration for her fifty years on the stage, she had been against it. Twenty-five of those years had been spent with Henry. If he had lived, he would have been celebrating his jubilee at the same time. The honor was as much due to him and the work they had done together as to her alone. Without him to share the triumph, half the pleasure would be gone. But people had persisted and now in spite of herself she could not help feeling little thrills of excitement. She had never thought that so many people from so many countries would have been willing to come to do her honor.

Duse, the great Italian actress, was making the journey from Florence, Coquelin and Réjane from France. Caruso, the famous tenor, whom she scarcely knew, had promised to sing.

Actors and actresses from all over England had been eager to appear in scenes, sketches, and tableaux. Messages of congratulation had begun to pour in from America, Canada, Australia, Germany, from countries which she had never even visited.

What a mammoth of a matinee, she thought with a gurgle of laughter when she arrived at the Drury Lane Theatre on June 12. It was to start at noon and would not finish until after six, barely in time for everyone to get away for the evening performance. One of the most delightful moments had been at two o'clock in the morning when she had visited the gallery queue waiting patiently through the night for the few remaining seats. They had given her a tumultuous reception.

The crowning event of the afternoon was the first act of *Much Ado about Nothing,* in which she was Beatrice once again, with Beerbohm Tree as Benedick, Forbes-Robertson as Claudio, and every available Terry in all the remaining parts: Marion, Kate, and Fred, and as many of the children as could be brought on as pages, torchbearers, dancers. Only the most loved one of all was not there. Teddy, who had designed the settings, was far away in Germany. The spoiled boy had reached maturity as an artist at last. He had published his book *On the Art of the Theatre,* and was beginning to win a world-wide reputation for his new and imaginative ideas on plays and their settings. She was immensely proud of him, even if it did mean that she saw less and less of him.

In her speech when the whole company were gathered around her on the vast Drury Lane stage, she said, "It is one of my chief joys today that I need not say goodbye—just yet—but can still speak to you as one who is still among you on the active list—still in your service—if you please."

THE NATIONAL PORTRAIT GALLERY

Ellen Terry at seventy-three, painted by W. G. Robertson

When it was all over, with everyone gone, and Edy had called a cab, there was still one more magical moment in that wonderful day. The gray-haired old cabby leaned down to peer at her before he broke into smiles. Once upon a time, he told them, fifty years ago, he had been in the habit of driving Mrs. Charles Kean home from the Princess Theatre and sometimes she used to give a lift to the two little Miss Terrys. For a moment the years rolled away. She was both the child Nellie and the famous actress of fifty-nine. Then they were jogging along to the Court Theatre, where she was appearing in *Captain Brassbound's Conversion.* It had taken Bernard Shaw ten years to persuade her to play the part he had created for her.

Afterwards it was home to her new flat in Chelsea. On the wall hung the portrait of Henry which had always been her favorite. The dark, dreaming eyes looked down at her with shrewd humor, the smile which had been the despair of the artist lurking around the determined mouth. Sometimes she would feel that she had never really left him.

A great many years still remained to her. She married again. James Carew was a young American from Indiana who had seen Ellen and Irving play in Chicago and had fallen in love with the theatre. He had come to England and studied hard to become an actor. He was in his early thirties, handsome and with a gentle, attractive manner. Ellen liked him at once when he came to play a small part in *Captain Brassbound's Conversion.* When she took the play to the United States, he went with her, this time as her leading man.

Ellen was lonely. For twenty-five years Henry Irving had been part of her life, a strong masculine prop on which she could rely. She missed his strength and his companionship. Carew was honest, straightforward, unpretentious. In the spring of 1907 they were married in Pittsburgh.

It was a rash decision. Carew had been enchanted by her beauty and charm, dazzled by her fame and popularity, and it was not until they returned to England that he realized the subordinate part he would play in her life. She had been independent too long. After two years there was a judicial separation, though a strong affection remained. They were warm friends for the rest of her life.

She was to play two more Shakespearean parts, Hermione in *The Winter's Tale* and the Nurse in *Romeo and Juliet*. When she found her memory failing, when it was difficult to learn the new, unfamiliar lines of modern dramatists, she began to lecture. Her material was the wisdom garnered from fifty years of interpreting Shakespeare's heroines.

To act you must make the written thing your very own, she would tell her young listeners. Beware of sound and fury signifying nothing. You must steal the words, steal the thought, and convey your stolen treasure to your audience with great art. She would break into a few lines of Beatrice, Juliet, Imogen, and the bare stage would be transformed. The enthralled public would be carried back into the theatre, hearing Shakespeare's words, fresh and golden, as if they had been newly minted that very morning.

She was never rich. She was far too generous. She gave with both hands, and there were many who asked her help. When Edy, anxious on her account, tried to step in and prevent the appeals from reaching her, she would make a little private list without Edy's knowledge, hurrying secretly to the post so that she should not fail those who depended on her.

In the stables at Smallhythe there was the wagonette with

Ellen, in her Nance Oldfield dress, and her grandchild Nelly (Teddy's daughter) in Ellen's garden at Tenterden, 1913. Ellen's signature dates from the time the picture was taken. Nelly's signature, so similar to her grandmother's, was put on the picture in the early 1960's

Ellen Terry at eighty-one

ARNOLD ROOD COLLECTION

its fat pony. When Teddy's children were there while their father was abroad, they all would bundle into the cart with the dogs and the kitten and off they would go for a day's picnic, coming back with baskets laden with flowers or nuts or blackberries. She still drove herself about the countryside in her pony trap. She never really cared for motor cars. They belonged to the cities, not to the slow rhythm of the country life she loved.

Her friends were legion and often from the younger generation. Her hair might be white, but there was about her something eternally youthful. When in 1925 she was made a Dame of the Grand Cross, she gurgled with delighted laughter. It was too absurd. How could anyone call her "Dame Ellen!" It made her feel old, she said.

Once after a supper party with some young friends she asked for a cab to be called, not a taxi but an old-fashioned "growler." All muffled up, spectacles on nose, she said, "Boost me in, dear boy."

And the cabby, peering down, said, "Ain't the lady as I 'ave the honor of drivin' Miss Ellen Terry? I ain't seen you, Mum, since *The Amber 'Eart*. 1887—I fink it was!"

"There now," she said in the golden voice which never lost its beauty. "There now! I told you I hadn't altered!"

And so it was until the end.

She died on July 21, 1928, in the early morning, with the sun shining, the jessamine and the honeysuckle climbing into the open windows of her simple bedroom at Smallhythe.

"No funeral gloom, my dears, when I am gone," she had written. The men from the fields left their work for an hour and gathered outside the church, their tools in their hands, to pay her a last tribute. She had always had a gay smile and a cheerful word for them all. When they carried her from Kent to London, the church bells rang out a merry peal and the people flocked the streets in holiday attire, tossing nosegays and bouquets before her as they had done in the great days at the Lyceum. At the funeral service the clear voices of the boy singers rose up in the hymn, "All things bright and beautiful."

"She had beauty, grace and genius but more wonderful still was her heart," wrote one of her oldest friends. "It was because she was all glorious within that she radiated happiness wherever she went."

"It is like a light going out," wrote another. "It had burned long and brightly, and had given everything it came near brightness, and some of its beauty."

Author's Note

IT HAS OFTEN BEEN SAID in criticism that, apart from Shakespeare, the plays produced by Henry Irving and Ellen Terry in their long reign at the Lyceum were no more than romantic melodramas. That statement fails to take into consideration the plain fact that during the mid-nineteenth century English drama, unlike poetry and the novel, was going through a bad period. Irving spent considerable sums of money commissioning playwrights to write for him, and very few of the works produced reached the required standard. Except for what were called the "cup and saucer" domestic comedies of Tom Robertson (1829–1871), theatre managers were almost entirely dependent on adaptations of popular novels, refurbishings of old plays, or translations from the French. It was not until the nineties that the plays of Arthur Pinero, Henry Arthur Jones, and Oscar Wilde began to appear, and even then, the best of the new drama was coming from abroad in Ibsen and Strindberg.

I feel it is worth remembering in Irving's defense that he produced three plays by the Poet Laureate Tennyson, one by Byron, and twelve by Shakespeare, restoring them for the first time in two hundred years to their original form. Another fact that must be borne in mind is that the Lyceum had to pay its way, unlike the National Theatre or the Royal Shakespeare Company of today, with which it may be compared. Even with substantial state subsidies and playing to full houses, these companies find it almost impossible to maintain their high standards and at the same time make a profit. How much more difficult it must have been at the Lyceum to support a large company and stage lavish productions entirely dependent on what came in at the box office. Only long runs of popular plays and the profits of provincial and American tours made it possible. The new controversial drama being written by Ibsen, Strindberg, and the young Bernard Shaw played to sparse audiences at tiny theatres. To have put it on at the Lyceum would have meant instant disaster.

It is interesting to note that the oil lamps and candles of an earlier age had been largely supplanted by gas lighting before 1827. At first it was heartily disliked by the actors, who complained bitterly that the heat of the flaring gas jets destroyed their makeup and melted the gum of their false beards and mustaches. By the skillful use of colored gauzes over wire guards, Irving contrived subtle and varied lighting effects. The first theatre to be lit entirely by electricity was the Savoy in 1881, where the Gilbert and Sullivan operas were staged. When the Lyceum was loaned to the American impresario, Augustin

Daly, in 1890, he introduced electricity. However, on her return to the theatre, Ellen disliked the harsh glare so much that she had no difficulty persuading Irving to restore gas. This was done and gas remained in use there until he left the theatre in 1902.

Teddy's work in the theatre was destined to have an immense influence on production methods throughout Europe and America. He is remembered more for the originality and visionary quality of his ideas than for actual achievement. He was more than thirty before he started to produce his brilliant writings, etchings, woodcuts, theatre designs, and scenic models. In 1905 he was invited to Berlin to produce Thomas Otway's *Venice Preserved.* In 1906 he designed settings for Ibsen's *Rosmersholm* starring Eleonora Duse, and in 1912 he directed *Hamlet* at the Moscow Art Theatre. He settled in Florence, where he founded and edited *The Mask*, a journal devoted to the art of the theatre, and ran a Theatre Workshop and School of Acting in the Arena Goldoni. His wife, May, divorced him after he went to Germany, and he later married Elena Meo, the daughter of an Italian musician, whom he met in England. He wrote lovingly and perceptively of his mother in *Ellen Terry and Her Secret Self* and later in *Henry Irving* paid tribute to the man whom he had always deeply admired. In 1957 at the age of eighty-five he was at last acknowledged by the English and he was made a Companion of Honour. He died in 1966.

Edy (Edith Ailsa Craig) toured America with her mother in 1907, acting as her stage manager. She designed costumes and founded a Sunday Play Society called the Pioneer Players. She had not her mother's charm or her ability to get on with everyone. Her critical spirit sometimes worked against her. She was severely practical and shouldered the financial responsibilities and care of her mother in her old age. In 1929 she instituted the annual Shakespearean Matinees, which took place in a converted barn in the garden at Smallhythe on the anniversary of Ellen Terry's death. One of her most interesting achievements was the creation of the Ellen Terry Museum, at Smallhythe, an invaluable collection of books, pictures, manuscripts, costumes, and theatrical properties, largely relating to Lyceum days. She died in 1947.

The Terry genius continued to flourish in many members of the family, notably in Fred Terry and his daughter, Phyllis Neilson Terry, and glows brilliantly today in Sir John Gielgud, Ellen's great-nephew, the grandson of her sister Kate.

Irving's elder son, Harry, developed into a creative actor of distinction, though he never achieved the fame of his father. His first notable success was in *The Admirable Crichton* by J. M. Barrie in 1902. Harry was a keen student of criminology and published a *Life of Judge Jeffreys* and *Studies of French Criminals.* He died in 1919.

Laurence, Irving's younger son, married a young actress, Mabel Hackney, and produced a number of foreign plays of distinction in London, including a translation of Dostoevsky's *Crime and Punishment.* On May 29, 1914, on the way back from a tour in Canada, he and his wife were drowned when the *Empress of Ireland* was rammed by a Norwegian collier and sank in thick fog in the Gulf of St. Lawrence.

A few notes about foreign actors mentioned in the text may be of interest.

SARAH BERNHARDT (1841–1923) made her debut at the Comédie Française in *Iphigénie en Aulide* in 1862. She was a dramatic actress of considerable power and personality, famous for her playing in Racine's *Phèdre* and *Andromaque* and Victor Hugo's *Hernani* and *Ruy Blas*. During the siege of Paris in the Franco-Prussian War she turned the Odéon Theatre into a hospital and organized an ambulance service. She made her first appearance in London in 1879 and in New York in 1880. She was a frequent guest of Irving's at the Lyceum.

ELEONORA DUSE (1859–1924) was an Italian actress who came from a family of actors and first appeared on the stage at the age of four. She made a great success in the plays of Gabriele d'Annunzio and Ibsen. It was said that to watch her act was like reading a psychological novel. In every role she was completely different, in contrast to Sarah Bernhardt, who never attempted to hide her own strong personality. Ellen admired Duse greatly and always saw her performances when Duse visited England. In later years Teddy, known professionally as Gordon Craig, was to design stage settings for her.

RÉJANE (1856–1920). Her real name was Gabrielle Charlotte Réju. She was a French actress of great emotional power, famous all over Europe in both tragedy and comedy, particularly in the plays of Sardou.

BENOÎT CONSTANT COQUELIN (1841–1909) was the son of a pastry cook. He made his name playing the comic servants in Molière's plays but during his long association with the Comédie Française also played tragic roles. He was Irving's guest at the Lyceum and was astonished at Ellen's natural acting, so different from the formal French style. "*Mais c'est charmant, elle a des vrais larmes aux yeux!*" he exclaimed, horrified at anyone shedding real tears on the stage. "The actor must in all circumstances remain the absolute master of himself and leave nothing to chance," was one of his own rules.

CHARLES ALBERT FECHTER (1824–1879) was an Englishman who had been brought up in France. In Paris he made his name as Armand in *La Dame aux Camélias* by Dumas *fils* and when he came to England created a sensation by playing a controversial Hamlet in a blond wig with Kate Terry as his Ophelia.

Bibliography

Benson, Frank, *My Memoirs*. London: Ernest Benn Ltd., 1930.

Carr, Alice Comyns, *Reminiscences*. London: William Heinemann Ltd., 1925.

Craig, Edward, *Gordon Craig*. New York: Alfred A. Knopf, 1968.

Craig, Edward Gordon, *Ellen Terry and Her Secret Self*. London: Samson, Low, Marston & Co., 1931.

———, *Henry Irving*. London: J. M. Dent & Sons, Ltd., 1930.

———, *Index to the Story of My Days*. New York: DBS Publications, 1957.

Harbron, Dudley, *The Conscious Stone*, a biography of Edward Godwin. London: Latimer House Ltd., 1949.

Hiatt, Charles, *Ellen Terry and Her Impersonations*. London: George Bell & Sons, Ltd., 1900.

Irving, Laurence, *Henry Irving*. London: Faber & Faber, Ltd., 1951.

———, *The Successors*. London: Rupert Hart-Davis, Ltd., 1967.

Manvell, Roger, *Ellen Terry*. New York: G. P. Putnam's Sons, 1968.

Nicoll, Allardyce, *A History of English Drama*, Vols. IV and V. New York: Cambridge University Press, 1959.

Robertson, W. Graham, *Time Was*. London: Hamish Hamilton, Ltd., 1931.

Shaw, George Bernard, *Dramatic Opinions and Essays*. London: Constable & Co. Ltd., 1931.

Steen, Margaret, *A Pride of Terrys*. London: Longmans, Green & Co. Ltd., 1962.

Stoker, Bram, *Personal Reminiscences of Henry Irving*. London: William Heinemann Ltd., 1906.

Terry, Ellen, *Memoirs*, edited by Edith Craig and Christopher St. John. London: Victor Gollancz Ltd., 1933.

———, *Four Lectures on Shakespeare*. London: Martin Hopkinson Ltd., 1932.

Index